NEW DIRECTIONS FOR TEACHING AND LEARNING

Robert J. Menges, *Northwestern University*
EDITOR-IN-CHIEF

Marilla D. Svinicki, *University of Texas, Austin*
ASSOCIATE EDITOR

Supplemental Instruction: Increasing Achievement and Retention

Deanna C. Martin
University of Missouri – Kansas City

David R. Arendale
University of Missouri – Kansas City

EDITORS

Number 60, Winter 1994

JOSSEY-BASS PUBLISHERS
San Francisco

SUPPLEMENTAL INSTRUCTION: INCREASING ACHIEVEMENT AND RETENTION
Deanna C. Martin, David R. Arendale (eds.)
New Directions for Teaching and Learning, no. 60
Robert J. Menges, Editor-in-Chief
Marilla D. Svinicki, Associate Editor

Microfilm copies of issues and articles are available in 16mm and 35mm,
as well as microfiche in 105mm, through University Microfilms Inc., 300
North Zeeb Road, Ann Arbor, Michigan 48106-1346.

LC 85-644763   ISSN 0271-0633   ISBN 0-7879-9999-7

NEW DIRECTIONS FOR TEACHING AND LEARNING is part of The Jossey-Bass
Higher and Adult Education Series and is published quarterly by Jossey-
Bass Inc., Publishers, 350 Sansome Street, San Francisco, California
94104-1342. Second-class postage paid at San Francisco, California, and
at additional mailing offices. POSTMASTER: Send address changes to New
Directions for Teaching and Learning, Jossey-Bass Inc., Publishers, 350
Sansome Street, San Francisco, California 94104-1342.

SUBSCRIPTIONS for 1994 cost $47.00 for individuals and $62.00 for institutions, agencies, and libraries.

EDITORIAL CORRESPONDENCE should be sent to the editor-in-chief, Robert J.
Menges, Northwestern University, Center for the Teaching Professions,
2003 Sheridan Road, Evanston, Illinois 60208-2610.

Cover photograph by Richard Blair/Color & Light © 1990.

Manufactured in the United States of America. Nearly all Jossey-Bass
books, jackets, and periodicals are printed on recycled paper that contains
at least 50 percent recycled waste, including 10 percent postconsumer
waste. Many of our materials are also printed with vegetable-based inks;
during the printing process, these inks emit fewer volatile organic compounds (VOCs) than petroleum-based inks. VOCs contribute to the formation of smog.

CONTENTS

About This Publication. Since 1980, *New Directions for Teaching and Learning (NDTL)* has brought a unique blend of theory, research, and practice to leaders in postsecondary education. *NDTL* sourcebooks strive not only for solid substance but also for timeliness, compactness, and accessibility.

The series has four goals: to inform readers about current and future directions in teaching and learning in postsecondary education, to illuminate the context that shapes these new directions, to illustrate these new directions through examples from real settings, and to propose ways in which these new directions can be incorporated into still other settings.

This publication reflects our view that teaching deserves respect as a high form of scholarship. We believe that significant scholarship is conducted not only by researchers who report results of empirical investigations but also by practitioners who share disciplined reflections about teaching. Contributors to *NDTL* approach questions of teaching and learning as seriously as they approach substantive questions in their own disciplines, and they deal not only with pedagogical issues but also with the intellectual and social context in which these issues arise. Authors deal on the one hand with theory and research and on the other with practice, and they translate from research and theory to practice and back again.

About This Volume. In this volume of *NDTL*, Deanna Martin, David Arendale, and their colleagues describe the development and uses of Supplemental Instruction in a range of settings. The concept of Supplemental Instruction involves identifying the learning processes and strategies that will help students master a given course and then making those processes part of the instruction itself. Supplemental Instruction has been used in institutions throughout the world and has helped untold numbers of students be successful where in the past they might have failed.

Robert J. Menges, *Editor-in-Chief*
Marilla D. Svinicki, *Associate Editor*

ROBERT J. MENGES, *editor-in-chief, is professor of education and social policy at Northwestern University, and senior researcher, National Center on Post-secondary Teaching, Learning, and Assessment.*

MARILLA D. SVINICKI, *associate editor, is director of the Center for Teaching Effectiveness, University of Texas at Austin.*

EDITORS' NOTES

When someone from Jossey-Bass contacted us to publish a monograph on Supplemental Instruction, our first thought was of our colleagues in developmental education, many of whom had extensive experience in institutions and with populations different from our own. We issued a call for papers for inclusion, and the response significantly exceeded our expectations. Unfortunately, in some instances we had to select from several papers which addressed similar issues, circumstances, or problems. We extend our personal thanks to those who submitted papers we did not use. Additionally, we wish to thank Drs. Sharon Bagg, Kay Blair, Ellen Forrest, Donald Mocker, Julia Visor, and Clark Chipman for their contributions to the development of VSI, which is based on Supplemental Instruction. We appreciate the assistance of Gloria Cristie and Karen Peace in preparing this manuscript, and Balaram Palasamudrum for his assistance in data analysis.

We developed the monograph with several audiences in mind. We wanted to provide a historical setting for institutions where Supplemental Instruction (SI) is being considered for adoption. For institutions where the program is already in place, we sought to deal with the kinds of issues that typically arise in discussion among developmental educators, faculty, and administration. For those seeking statistical validation of the SI model, we aspired to present objective data. For those in regional leadership roles, we tried to underline and highlight the bottom line by addressing cost effectiveness.

Organically, the monograph fell logically into three sections. In the first section, we describe the origin of SI and answer these questions:

- What insight conceived SI?
- What problem did SI originally address?
- Why did SI expand its focus from a retention program for students in health science professional schools to undergraduate first- and second-year students?
- What are the typical start-up steps in establishing SI?
- What can SI contribute to faculty development?

For our first chapter, we asked vice chancellor Gary Widmar, the University of Missouri–Kansas City (UMKC) chief administrative officer over the SI program since its inception, to share his experience in an institution which for the first time faced high attrition, first-generation university students, and faculty opposition to both remedial education and developmental studies. In that environment, SI was invented. Chapter Two contains David Arendale's view of the evolutionary history of SI from the health science professional schools to the undergraduate campus. David also sets SI in its original theoretical and philosophical contexts. Len Ainsworth and his colleagues reflected on their start-up experience and contributed their beginners' guide, which became Chapter Three. Sherrin Marshall, who extended SI into faculty development, takes us with her as she deals with initial faculty responses, overcomes primary roadblocks, implements the program, and documents changes in faculty perspectives.

The next set of chapters views applications of SI in and across various content disciplines. In Sandra Zerger's chapter, theoretical and operational aspects are viewed from the contemporary perspective, along with a discussion of the importance of epistemology and axiology of the discipline which SI is meant to supplement. Chapter Six, an application of SI to mathematics by Sandra Burmeister and colleagues, provides a brief discursion into peer collaborative learning. Collaboration arises again in the application of SI to the chemistry class in Chapter Seven by Nancy Lockie and Robert Van Lanen. Chapter Eight authors Patricia Kenney and James Kallison, Jr., conducted research on course grades in college-level calculus courses with SI. The effectiveness of SI with lower ability students in the calculus course appeals particularly to those who are concerned with such developmental issues as mathematics literacy.

In the final chapter, Deanna Martin and Robert Blanc provide a look at one direction SI might move toward in the future as students begin to exercise some control over the pace of the lecture delivery. SI may emerge as the basis for an alternative to the noncredit developmental curriculum that is currently losing favor among some educators who voice concerns about high drop and failure rates.

Those of us who are responsible for dissemination of the SI model know how deeply indebted all developmental educators are to those who have taken SI in new directions and who have taken the time to document what they did. Those seeking evidence of peer collaboration need look no further than the SI users' network to verify the power of shared experience.

Deanna C. Martin
David R. Arendale
Editors

DEANNA C. MARTIN is director of the Center for Academic Development and professor in the School of Education at the University of Missouri–Kansas City.

DAVID R. ARENDALE is national project director for Supplemental Instruction and associate director of the Center for Academic Development at the University of Missouri–Kansas City.

A historical review of the development and implementation of Supplemental Instruction is presented by the chief student affairs officer at the University of Missouri–Kansas City.

Supplemental Instruction: From Small Beginnings to a National Program

Gary E. Widmar

Historical Context for Supplemental Instruction

People who pioneer new territory travel paths filled with quicksand and more than a few pitfalls. After an organization develops and validates a program, others often wonder how they can avoid those hazards and where they can find the passes through the mountains of opposition. A map of how Supplemental Instruction (SI) evolved might prove useful to those who are considering student retention from a campus-wide perspective.

As chief executive officer for the Supplemental Instruction program, I have had the opportunity to be personally involved in its growth and development since SI began twenty years ago. I have also met most of the faculty, staff members, and administrators from other campuses who come to UMKC to participate in the SI workshops and training programs. I have been particularly mindful of the questions and concerns these professionals bring with them. In this paper, I combine my answers to the most commonly asked questions with my sense of the gestation and maturation of a unique educational endeavor.

The impetus for developing SI began in 1963. At that time, the University of Kansas City (UKC) was a small, private university. During its development, UKC acquired independent, freestanding professional schools of law, dentistry, pharmacy, and a conservatory of music. As the University of Missouri reached out to the urban centers of the State, these disparate elements were forged into a single entity, the University of Missouri–Kansas City (UMKC).

As a public institution, the newly reorganized UMKC faced some difficult changes. One of the first was a result of the change in patterns of student access to the university. Instead of limiting the student clientele to the top 20 percent of the high-school graduating class as had previously been the case, the university now offered admission to a much more culturally and academically diverse population. This change was particularly difficult for many of the faculty from Ivy League universities who had taken positions here precisely because the student population tended to be very well prepared for the rigors of academic study.

Predictably, the first disturbing aftermath of the transition was a high attrition rate that rose from 20 to 45 percent among entering students. The university formed several committees to investigate this phenomenon. In typical committee fashion, they explored and rejected many options over the next several years without arriving at a consensus.

In 1972, I received a telephone call from the associate provost for the health sciences, who was particularly interested in responding to the attrition problems among the minority students in our schools of medicine, pharmacy, and dentistry. He had just received a grant of $7,000 from a local foundation to deal with this specific retention issue and offered me the opportunity to develop some type of program for this population.

Knowing little about academic support services, but reluctant to turn down funds that could benefit students, I searched the campus for assistance. Deanna Martin, then a graduate student in reading education who was teaching a freshman level reading and study skills course, accepted my offer of an assistantship in student affairs. I asked her to work with highly skilled, carefully selected minority students who, for some unexplained reason, were unable to achieve in the health science schools.

Martin, also staff resource person to the primary retention committee, conducted a survey of the research on retention and investigated how other campuses resolved this problem. Through her research, Martin provided the committee with an awareness of the issues and offered potential solutions that might prove beneficial.

A telephone survey of learning center directors revealed the most useful information about current academic assistance programs. The 1970 survey indicated most of the learning centers had created drop-in, crisis-oriented programs. Most of their clientele were students experiencing some kind of academic difficulty, for example, a poor grade on a major assignment or exam.

According to the interview data, directors of programs across the nation voiced several common concerns. One major concern was the feeling of being ancillary to the mainstream values of the institutions they served. They also described themselves as being accorded little recognition and limited respect. In addition, they complained that universities used their centers as the "dumping ground" for all the academic problems. These directors found diagnostic and standardized tests insufficient to predict which students would need assistance, and their services were often "too little, too late." Following are other issues raised in the interviews:

They described the regularly scheduled remedial and developmental courses as "add-ons" to otherwise heavy class loads.
They could not demonstrate that students actually transferred the skills they learned to regular courses.
They reported that those students most in need of assistance avoided asking for help in a timely fashion, because they did not want to be stigmatized or labeled remedial.
The individual tutoring that they all offered was expensive, and many students failed to keep scheduled appointments.
Evaluation of the effectiveness of services was very difficult.
Financial support from the institution was tenuous.

After reviewing this information, the committee reached a consensus for perhaps the first time: any program implemented at UMKC must be rigorously evaluated and cost effective. As part of her research, Martin observed Martha Maxwell, then director of the Learning Center on the Berkeley campus of the University of California, whose program demonstrated that gifted students did indeed benefit from academic support services. Martin returned with a particularly valuable insight: skills instruction is best accomplished if applied to specific content. After completing her research, Martin designed the SI program and piloted it in the School of Dentistry in the early 1970s. Fortunately, the first year produced positive preliminary results.

The SI pilot addressed some of the committee members' more basic concerns. Administrators and faculty both sought a program that would reduce attrition without lowering academic standards or inflating grades. Since minimal campus resources would be available, the administration required a program that was cost effective, measurable through tight evaluations, and acceptable to the faculty. The faculty wanted a program that had a nonremedial image, required no extra work on their part, and promoted independent learning. Students needed a program that would neither stigmatize nor label them. The retention committee wanted to balance the often conflicting needs of students, faculty, and administrators.

Committee members thought that the SI program might meet these various concerns; therefore, they agreed to lend their verbal support to an expanded SI pilot. SI won an award from the Health Careers Opportunities Program (U.S. Department of Health, Education, and Welfare) that allowed SI to expand into UMKC's schools of Dentistry, Medicine, and Pharmacy. With an additional local grant from the Kansas City Association of Trusts and Foundations, the original local funder, SI increased its scope to include the College of Arts and Sciences. At that time, its potential as a campus-wide program became apparent.

In 1981, after nine years of applications and refinements, the SI program won certification by the U.S. Department of Education as an *Exemplary Educational Program*. With this award, SI became eligible for funds from the National Diffusion Network, which the staff used to help other universities implement the SI model. To date, UMKC has trained learning assistance personnel and faculty from over 400 colleges and universities in Supplemental Instruction.

Problems in Implementing Supplemental Instruction

It is not unusual for some faculty to be reluctant to invest in a retention program. Certainly, not everyone welcomed the idea of providing organized academic support at UMKC. Some faculty believed that retention programs were either unnecessary or inappropriate at an institution, such as UMKC, which is directed toward graduate and professional education. Forty-five percent of the 10,000 students fit those categories, and the average age of students at UMKC is twenty-eight. The faculty's first overt argument derived from their preference for working with students at advanced levels. That argument was essentially this: since academic support programs target primarily beginning students, and since UMKC does not have many of those, why would the university want to be involved in a retention program?

Some faculty argued that students who cannot perform satisfactorily should attend less rigorous colleges and universities. Many felt strongly that if admission standards were higher, there would be no need for retention programs. Others expressed the fear that SI might infringe upon academic freedom by promoting lowered standards and grade inflation. One faculty member was suspicious when the university offered the SI program at no apparent additional cost and expressed concern over possible ulterior motives behind the program.

The faculty who expressed the greatest interest in SI tended to be those who had reputations for teaching tough but fair courses. Typically other faculty and students regarded them as strong teachers who were helpful to students but uncompromising in their academic rigor. In the end, faculty positivists did defer to the data, which demonstrated clearly that selection procedures were imperfect: students predicted to succeed sometimes demonstrated unexpected weaknesses, while some who were regarded as weak proved successful.

Faculty also found that the SI program did not require them to change either their teaching strategies or grading standards. Further, SI did not take additional time. In fact, it often saved time as the SI leader helped students with simple questions or study skills needs, thus freeing the instructor to spend time with students who had content concerns. Moreover, through monitoring the students' progress, the SI leader could provide faculty with feedback on what their students found problematic.

It was fortuitous that SI began in the health sciences schools. Those schools attracted our most carefully selected population and probably the brightest students. This fact, paired with the success of SI both in retaining our target population and in improving academic performance across the board, allowed me to say to other deans and faculty, "If SI works in the medical school or the dental school, given their makeup, how could it not work in your academic field, which is not as highly selective?" From that time on, my role has been that of the advocate, the eliminator of political roadblocks, the resource finder, and the public relations person who tries to keep the administration and faculty cognizant of the success of SI and responsive to the changes that have resulted from the SI program.

Supplemental Instruction and the Office of Student Affairs

Curiously enough, despite its modest beginnings and almost absurd allocation of $7,000, SI was to have a clear impact on the entire Division of Student Affairs. To see how this happened, it is necessary to let a few skeletons out of our academic closet.

The simple fact is this: on our campus, as on other campuses, student affairs programs have always had less prestige than academic affairs programs and consequently less funding. On our campus, research receives the greatest homage. There are other campuses where teaching is honored. In both types of institutions, divisions of student affairs have sometimes been seen as a necessary but not necessarily valued endeavor, and those activities which center on research or instruction have more secure funding bases. Consequently, when administration must tighten the budget, student services and programs tend to become quick targets for deeper cuts than those activities deemed more central to the research and instructional missions of the institution.

In the Division of Student Affairs at UMKC, we have always argued that our programs are cocurricular rather than extracurricular, that the research and instructional programs would be short-lived without the support of our offices, and my academic colleagues would grant that the institution would be hard to manage without student records, but that "The faculty and the library are the heart and soul of the institution." The unspoken implication assigns to Student Affairs the more remote anatomical segments.

As SI developed, the academics on campus began to acknowledge our claim to cocurricular status. First, the data base demonstrated that the typical student who participated in SI performed at a higher level than the student who did not, and course grade distribution changed significantly. The percentage of successful students in classes increased, and a greater number of "A" students surfaced. When we unveiled that information, faculty began to take us seriously. We were dealing not with Greeks but with grades; not with sports but with scholarship. The continually expanding data base of SI has established the clear relevance of SI to the research and instructional missions of UMKC. Subsequently, other programs within the Division of Student Affairs have subjected their activities to rigorous evaluation. These efforts have enabled us to interface with the academic side of the university on a more common and equal footing. We had entered the arena where research, results, and data are paramount, where people and programs are judged on the basis of their statistical significance. We now had "P" value!

As vice chancellor of student affairs, I have both the privilege and the responsibility to establish funding priorities within my division. I make no secret of the fact that some of our programs are going to be immune from major reductions. If I am forced to make cuts, SI is not going to be a likely candidate. I believe the retention record of SI demonstrates the value of the program to the institution. On the other hand, I must acknowledge that if I were on the academic side, I might not accord SI the same priority. I might find it difficult to justify retaining students at the expense of a key faculty position, for example. These considerations lead me to conclude that placing Supplemental Instruction under the aegis of student affairs gave the embryonic program a buffer against budget cuts.

Financing Supplemental Instruction

Many administrators assume that they must allocate some measure of discretionary campus wealth to begin an academic support program like SI. That was certainly not the case at UMKC, nor does it have to be the case elsewhere. At UMKC we estimate conservatively that SI's return to the institution is approximately $1.50 for each dollar invested. This figure is based upon the evidence of increased student reenrollment and persistence toward graduation. It also factors in all administrative and instructional costs. The staff estimates the initial cost per course of implementing SI at $900, which covers the SI leader's salary, books, and photocopying costs. The same amount, spent for individual tutoring, would be a scant resource indeed.

Currently, the SI program probably earns greater national renown than most of the programs on this campus. As a data-driven program that can be promoted on the basis of its outcome measures, SI holds special attractiveness for administrators. SI requires neither theoretical, political, nor emotional defense as a program that will benefit students; instead, SI finds statistical, factual support. At UMKC we were meticulous about our data collection and analyses, and that exacting care warranted the academic and pedagogical acceptance of the faculty.

Supplemental Instruction and National Trends in Education

Martin's 1972 research on student support programs concluded that no one in American higher education appeared to have a comprehensive retention plan powerful enough to affect the attrition problems faced by institutions with diverse student populations. That realization came as a considerable surprise to the Retention Committee.

Certainly over the last two decades, the whole arena of retention has become a growing concern. While federal funding has changed its focus from specific support for minority retention to retention of economically disadvantaged populations, the questions and concerns of faculty and administrators have remained fairly consistent. At a very basic level, it is more cost effective to retain existing students than to recruit new ones. Competition is high for postsecondary students, and some institutions operate on a slim margin. Therefore, retention efforts need to be broad in their reach and integrated into the academic and social culture of the institution.

It is important to note that in-house SI research verifies that UMKC loses not only academically underprepared students; we also lose some who are among the most prepared. At the undergraduate level, when we look at exit interviews and questionnaire data on why students leave, the prepared students do not identify themselves as leaving because of academic difficulty, nor do their grades identify them as leaving for academic reasons. Closer inspection, however, reveals that C grades devastate some students who expect A's just as much as D's and F's devastate marginal students. Both groups leave, and both take their tuition with them. Research on SI attendance shows that more high- and mid-range students return to the university in subsequent semesters; therefore, participation in SI appears related to the retention rate of our better students as well as those who may be struggling.

Support for Continued Supplemental Instruction

Faculty and administrators frequently wonder how a university can justify supporting a large SI program during economically difficult times. Those reasons are presented below.

SI Supports Cultural Diversity. For students who come from rather narrow backgrounds, SI provides a pluralistic environment where they can learn to value the unique perceptions of others who may view the world differently. In this way, SI has been effective in integrating students of varying ability levels and backgrounds into a common class.

SI Supports Critical Thinking. Part of the training that SI leaders receive emphasizes learning strategies designed to foster critical thinking and reasoning skills. The SI leader encourages students to question and seek verification of their ideas, discuss and analyze course content, clarify and enhance their understanding of what they read and learn, figure out learning strategies that are the most productive, and generally learn how to tell the difference between what they do and do not understood. These experiences help students become more powerful thinkers and learners.

SI Supports Retention and Performance. Research at UMKC and other campuses across the United States, and more recently abroad, attests to the effectiveness of SI in increasing student performance, reducing course attrition, and promoting enrollment in subsequent semesters. At UMKC, there is a positive correlation between SI participation and graduation rates.

It is also worth noting that SI works well across the range of campus programs from entry-level arts and sciences courses to advanced courses in professional schools and across various institutional types: private institutions; public institutions; community colleges; and research universities in developed and in developing countries. This is not a support program designed for a specific special interest group.

SI Is Both Replicable and Adaptable. One of the advantages to institutions is that Supplemental Instruction offers an identifiable, structured program or model. Unlike "collaborative learning," "cooperative learning," "writing across the curriculum," or "cultural diversity," *Supplemental Instruction* is not an amorphous term. The concepts underlying these other phrases find definition in the practice of the professionals who are applying them to their own classes, and in practice these definitions lack consistency. Thus, any evaluation of the effect of applying a concept is practically impossible.

That is not the case with SI. If a campus wants to implement the model, a USDOE-supported training program is offered at UMKC. The three-day training program includes materials for campus use, and all participants have access to technical assistance from the UMKC Center and from certified trainers in the field who have had advanced SI training and experience.

SI is also adaptable. Programs developed at one institution may need to be tailored with specific characteristics. With a history of fifteen years of helping staff from other institutions adapt the SI program, one of SI's strengths is the wealth of insight it can access with respect to variations that people might wish to try. The staff can, in most cases, access individuals who have either experimented with an alteration or who have it in place.

SI enjoys a strong network of hundreds of users who are regularly adding their own experiences and research to the growing data base and literature. Many individuals have invested their time and resources in the SI program and have helped its founders grow in their understanding of the program's value and use. The U.S. Department of Education has revalidated and funded Supplemental Instruction for a third time, and SI stands as testimony to the effectiveness of the endeavors of those at UMKC and other institutions to ensure success for students who might otherwise be lost along the pathway to meeting their educational goals.

GARY E. WIDMAR *is vice chancellor for student affairs and professor of education at the University of Missouri–Kansas City.*

A framework for understanding Supplemental Instruction is presented along with theoretical and philosophical underpinnings.

Understanding the Supplemental Instruction Model

David R. Arendale

Overview of Supplemental Instruction

Supplemental Instruction (SI) is a student academic assistance program that increases academic performance and retention through its use of collaborative learning strategies. The SI program targets traditionally difficulty academic courses, those that typically have 30 percent or higher rate of D or F final course grades or withdrawals, and provides regularly scheduled, out-of-class, peer-facilitated sessions that offer students an opportunity to discuss and process course information (Martin, Lorton, Blanc, and Evans, 1977).

High-Risk Courses Versus High-Risk Students. SI thus avoids the remedial stigma often attached to traditional academic assistance programs, since it does not identify *high-risk students* but identifies *high-risk classes*. SI is open to all students in the targeted course; therefore, prescreening of students is unnecessary. Since the SI program begins the first week of the academic term, the program provides academic assistance during the critical initial six-week period of class before many students face their first major examination. Attrition is highest during this period (Blanc, DeBuhr, and Martin, 1983; Noel, Levitz, and Saluri, 1985).

Historically difficult or high-risk courses often share the following characteristics: large amounts of weekly readings from both difficult textbooks and secondary library reference works, infrequent examinations that focus on higher cognitive levels of Bloom's taxonomy, voluntary and unrecorded class attendance, and large classes in which each student has little opportunity for interaction with the professor or the other students. SI is often attached to traditionally difficult, high-risk courses that serve first- and second-year students. Several institutions report the successful use of SI with students in graduate and professional schools (Bridgham and Scarborough, 1992; Martin and Arendale, 1992; Martin, 1980). However, each institution may develop its own definition of *high-risk courses.*

Such a designation of high-risk for a course makes no prejudicial comment about the professor or the students. It is a numerical calculation that indicates a sizeable number of students have difficulty in meeting academic requirements for the class. Rather than blaming the students or the professor, the designation suggests that additional academic support is needed for students to raise their level of academic performance to meet the level deemed appropriate by the classroom professor. In recent years, the popular and professional literature has been replete with extensive discussions about who is at fault for the perceived lower quality of student academic achievement. SI bypasses this issue and provides a practical solution that helps students meet the professor's level of expectation.

Proactive Assistance Before Problems Occur. Assistance begins in the first week of the term. The SI leader introduces the program during the first class session and surveys the students to establish a schedule for the SI sessions. Attendance is voluntary. Students of varying abilities participate, and no effort is made to segregate students based on academic ability. Many underprepared students who might otherwise avoid seeking assistance will participate in SI since it is not perceived to be remediation and there is no stigma attached. Such stigma can cause motivation problems for developmental students (Somers, 1988).

SI enables students to master course content while they develop and integrate effective learning and study strategies. Therefore, learning/study strategies (for example, note-taking, organization, test preparation) are integrated into the course content during the SI sessions. Immediate practice and reinforcement of these acquired skills are provided. SI collaborative sessions capitalize on the use of the "teachable moment" to apply the learning strategies to the course material. Educational researchers (Dimon, 1988; Keimig, 1983; Stahl, Simpson, and Hayes, 1992) have concluded that it is difficult to teach transferable study skills in isolation from content material.

Features of SI That Contribute to Student Success. Several features of the SI model operate to influence higher levels of student academic performance. The impact of Supplemental Instruction can be quantified by positive differences in student performance and retention rates. The following factors are most often mentioned by SI staff as well as by participating faculty and students (Martin and others, 1983)

The service is proactive rather than reactive. SI schedules are set during the first week of class, allowing students to obtain assistance before they encounter academic difficulty. Most "early alert" retention programs are not triggered until the student has already earned a "D" or "F" on a major examination.

The service is attached directly to specific courses. Reading, learning, and study skills instruction are offered in the context of course requirements and as an outgrowth of student questions and concerns. Thus instruction has immediate application. While many students may self-report their need for academic assistance, only a small group will voluntarily attend workshops that feature instruction in isolated study skills.

SI leaders attend all class sessions. Such attendance contrasts sharply with the more common tutorial practice of providing instruction based largely upon the student's perceptions of what occurred in class. Student perceptions are often distorted as well as time-consuming to report during the academic assistance sessions.

By design, SI is not a remedial program. Although SI is effective with under-prepared students, it is not viewed as remedial. The students who are most likely to volunteer initially are those who tend to be better prepared academically. The willingness of this group to participate encourages the participation of less able students who often find it difficult to admit that they need assistance.

SI sessions are designed to promote a high degree of student interaction and mutual support. Such interaction leads to the formation of peer study groups and facilitates the mainstreaming of culturally diverse as well as disadvantaged students. SI has relied upon the power of group study for the past twenty years, long before the current trend of promoting collaborative learning groups in higher education.

SI provides an opportunity for the course instructor to receive useful feedback from the SI leader. Students generally hesitate to be candid about academic concerns to course instructors for fear of demeaning themselves or offending the professor. They will, however, openly acknowledge their problems to the SI leader. The duty of the SI leader is to listen to their comments and then to redirect the students toward developing strategies to cope with the situation. The SI leader is not to assess the course professor or agree or disagree with student comments. If the course professor has previously invited feedback from the SI leader, the SI leader shares student comments or concerns in a nonthreatening and anonymous fashion, privately with the course instructor.

When SI May Be Less Effective. While success varies among and between SI programs, we have no data that would suggest any major limitations in SI. We do know, however, that conducting SI is more challenging in content areas where prerequisite skills are a key variable.

For example, if students do not remember any algebra, they will have a particularly difficult time in chemistry. SI can be and is effective in these areas. However, SI leaders must invest more time in planning. SI sessions often need to last longer than fifty minutes to cover additional material and provide additional time for students to practice and master the course material and study strategies. Additionally, SI groups may need to be reorganized to ensure that leaders who review the basics of algebra do not bore the more mathematically able students.

Our experience has been that SI is least effective when it is attached to remedial classes. First, students may refuse to attend SI sessions if they do not perceive the course to be demanding. Second, SI has not been effective for students who cannot read, take lecture notes, write, or study at the high school level. Therefore, we stress that adopting institutions use SI in nonremedial settings with high-risk, demanding courses.

We have also found that the SI model needs to be slightly modified in courses that are problem-based and involve practice for mastery. In those circumstances, SI sessions need to be more frequent and sometimes longer. For example, a three-credit-hour accounting course might require sufficient SI sessions to allow for the review of various types of problems, or a calculus class might require extended sessions to allow time for modeling and practice so that students become proficient problem solvers.

Key SI Program Personnel. Key people involved with SI on each campus include the SI leaders, the SI supervisor, and the course instructors. Each plays an important role in creating the environment that allows the SI program to flourish.

With the increasing diversity in the college classroom and in the level of student academic preparedness, institutions are seeking to develop a community of learners. SI helps promote the formation of such communities and promotes scholarship through increased academic performance and retention of students. Faculty enjoy the resources and support provided by the SI leader.

The SI leader. The SI leader is a student who has successfully completed the targeted class or a comparable course. It is ideal if the student has taken the course from the same instructor for whom he or she is now providing SI assistance. The SI leader is trained in proactive learning and study strategies and operates as a "model student," attending all course lectures, taking notes, and reading all assigned materials. The SI leader conducts three or more out-of-class SI sessions per week during which he or she integrates "how to learn" with "what to learn" (Martin and others, 1983).

The SI leader is a facilitator, not a mini-professor. The role of the leader is to provide structure to the study session, not relecture or introduce new material. The SI leader should be a "model student" who shows how successful students think about and process course content. He or she facilitates a process of collaborative learning, an important strategy since it helps students to empower themselves rather than remain dependent as they might in traditional tutoring. Research suggests that tutoring relationships do not always promote transfer of needed academic skills (Blanc, DeBuhr, and Martin, 1983; Dimon, 1988; Keimig, 1983; Martin and Arendale, 1990, 1992; Martin and Gravina, 1990; Martin and others, 1983; Martin and Blanc, 1981; Martin, 1980; Martin, Lorton, Blanc, and Evans, 1977; Maxwell, 1990).

A central responsibility of the SI leader is to integrate study skills with the course content. As someone who has performed well in the course, the SI leader has displayed mastery of the course material. However, it is important that the SI leader share his or her learning strategies with the other students in the SI sessions. If the students learn only content material and not the underlying study strategies, they will have a high probability of experiencing academic difficulty in succeeding courses.

The integration of study skills with the course content is a key difference between SI and other forms of collaborative learning. It is not just that students are working together; rather, it is the planned integration and practice of study strategies that sets SI apart. We believe that by combining *what to learn* with *how to learn it*, students are able to develop both content competency and transferable academic skills that pay off in higher grades during future academic terms.

The SI supervisor. The SI supervisor is an on-site professional staff person who implements the SI program and supervises the SI leader. The supervisor is responsible for identifying the targeted courses, gaining faculty support, selecting and training leaders, and monitoring and evaluating the program. Supervisors meet with SI leaders weekly during the term as a group or individually. Supervisors of most programs have formal meetings with all SI leaders together at least three times during the term for follow-up and problem solving.

SI supervisors attend a three and one-half day training workshop covering the areas of implementation and management, training, supervision, evaluation, and study strategies. Continued professional development is available through professional development seminars.

The faculty member. The third key person in implementing SI is the faculty member who teaches the course in which SI is offered. Faculty screen SI leaders for content competency. SI leaders are encouraged to meet weekly with SI course faculty members during their office hours to discuss SI session activities. Faculty cooperation is an essential ingredient of the SI model; therefore, SI is only used in classes where professors understand and support the idea. This policy holds true even if department chairs and deans request that SI be attached to certain classes.

While regular meetings are encouraged, faculty are free to choose their level of involvement with the SI leaders and the program supervisor. Some faculty members choose to meet with the SI leader to plan for SI sessions. This may include the creation of work sheets, mock examinations, or other materials. Many other faculty also request that the SI leader provide anonymous feedback from students concerning difficulties encountered during class lectures or with the reading materials. On the other hand, some faculty choose not to devote additional time to the program.

The SI program staff makes every effort to be supportive of the professor. This support might include checking the bookstore to see that the number of textbooks is sufficient to accommodate the number enrolled; calling students who are absent; checking materials on reserve in the library; and handing out materials during class. The only restrictions placed on SI leaders are that they may not share the SI session attendance sheets nor help create or grade course examinations.

Creating Awareness and Generating Support for SI on Campus

Gaining acceptance for any new student support program has historically been a difficult undertaking, especially in times of limited resources. Additionally, since the impetus for new academic support programs often comes from administrators or student affairs staff, there is the risk of potential opposition among the faculty.

Our experience (Martin and others, 1983), as well as reports from other institutions that have adopted SI, lead us to the following four suggestions for generating on-campus program support:

It is essential, our experience demonstrates, that facilitators receive *training* in the use of the SI program. While the basic tenets of SI programs are relatively simple, integration of course content review with study strategy practice and implementation is more complex. Issues and activities often covered during training workshops include mock SI session participation, SI session supervision, SI leader training topics, data collection and analysis activities, strategies to promote the SI program, and other practical issues related to program implementation and growth.

Such workshops are held in Kansas City and at a variety of locations across the United States, providing an opportunity to not only receive helpful training, but also to meet with other institutions that are also present for the workshop. SI has continued to grow and evolve for the last two decades in part because of the interaction between other adopting institutions.

Our second recommendation for generating on-campus support is to have a *pilot program* approach to starting SI. The best way to generate on-campus support is to have a successful pilot in place. Faculty members who have had positive experiences with SI become the program's strongest advocates.

We advise adopting institutions to begin a pilot program by eliciting the *support* of one or two faculty members who are well respected by their peers and teach entry level courses that are traditionally difficult for students. These faculty should have reputations as excellent instructors who have both rigorous and fair grading standards. They should also be willing to assign a higher than normal distribution of A, B, and C grades if students display increased levels of performance on examinations.

Our final suggestion for generating support for SI concerns the data collected. After conducting the pilot program, it is critical to prepare and disseminate *final reports* on the outcomes. Part of the attraction of SI to administrators and faculty members is the analysis of hard data—final course grades of SI participants compared with nonparticipants. Such reports are also helpful in presenting the findings to other faculty who may be interested in attaching SI to their courses. We suggest that faculty be approached individually, in small groups, or in departmental meetings. The SI supervisor should invite the instructors who were involved in the pilot to be part of these presentations.

When Supplemental Instruction has been carried out on other campuses without a pilot program to generate initial on-campus support (for example, when SI has been mandated by an administrator), the service has proven less than successful. Once faculty concerns are made public, they are difficult to address adequately, and attempts to do so are often viewed with skepticism. On the other hand, if SI is willingly piloted with a school or department, the program will generate its own support. One final note: while the UMKC SI program has not been a success with all students who have tried it, we have yet to lose a single faculty member!

Different Approaches to Assisting Students

Robert Blanc, associate professor and curriculum specialist for the School of Medicine at the University of Missouri–Kansas City, should be credited with the conceptual framework for comparing and contrasting the traditional (medical) and nontraditional approaches to assisting students.

Traditional Approaches to Assisting Students. Traditional individual tutorial practices may be described as following a medical model: an individual is identified as needing professional assistance on the basis of (a) prior history and diagnostic testing, (b) self-referral in response to perceived symptoms, or (c) referral by another professional in response to observed symptoms.

In some institutions, identification of high-risk students is based primarily on prior history of test scores (a). These tertiary institutions are likely to be somewhat selective, requiring students to submit to extensive prematriculation testing and interviews. Professional schools and private, selective colleges are among those fitting this category. Students entering such institutions typically commit for the long term and, at a minimum, can be expected to persist for a year. Under these circumstances, academic therapy with students at risk can begin immediately upon matriculation and can continue until students give evidence of being able to function independently in the academic environment.

As noted (b), some students voluntarily seek assistance. Their symptoms in these instances may range from free-floating anxiety in the academic setting to unsatisfactory performance in one or more highly specific settings. The tutor or resource specialist must function first as diagnostician, identifying the basis for the students' self-referral and differentiating between anxiety and a variety of other reasons for unsatisfactory performance. Having established at least a tentative diagnosis, the tutor then becomes the therapist, helping students to negotiate the academic demands of the institution.

Finally, another professional, usually a professor or graduate teaching assistant, may become aware that a student is in academic difficulty (c). This awareness may come in a variety of ways, most likely in the wake of unsuccessful performance on an academic task. For example, the faculty member may refer the student for tutorial assistance to correct an academic problem apparent because of a low test score. In this instance, the tutor functions, as described previously, first as a diagnostician and then as a therapist.

Rationale for a Nontraditional Approach. It was in a milieu dominated by tutorial services in the medical model that SI developed. The developers at UMKC found that several assumptions of the medical model either did not apply or were not practiced in their institution. Subsequent adoption of SI on other campuses may suggest that the same assumptions were found wanting on these other campuses as well.

As noted, the traditional model relies on identification of the "high-risk" student, the student deemed deficient or "at-risk" in some way. In institutions other than those described, that is, selective tertiary and professional schools, several factors preclude such prematriculation identification.

First, the faculty and staff must know entering students in time for key personnel to establish contact with at-risk students. Second, they must note in this context that neither prior performance nor standardized testing is sufficiently reliable as a prediction criterion of who is and is not at-risk. As many as 50 percent of those whose prior scores suggest they are at-risk prove to be successful without intervention, and many of those who are not identified in this manner prove to be unsuccessful.

Analyses of high school grades and standardized college entrance examinations do not identify all students who will drop out of college for academic reasons (Blanc, DeBuhr, and Martin, 1983; Christie and Dinham, 1991; Martin and others, 1983; Tinto, 1987), and attrition cannot be addressed effectively by providing help only to those students who show either symptoms or predisposing weaknesses. The treatment must be more generalized, and the problem must be addressed at or near its source: the mismatch between the level of instruction and the level of student preparation (Martin, Lorton, Blanc, and Evans, 1977).

Timely identification of students who are at-risk is difficult in the traditional model. Faculty who can refer students for corrective instruction are rarely able to make a referral before the scoring of the first course examination. Students who are referred after that time are at a considerable disadvantage, trying to catch up with the class after a very poor start. The rate of student attrition across courses is greatest in the first six weeks or after the first exam when students may find their grades disappointing (Blanc, DeBuhr, and Martin, 1983; Noel, Levitz, and Saluri, 1985).

Students who are at risk are among those least compliant with faculty recommendations for special help, whether for personal counseling or for academic assistance. Such students often perceive that tutorial help, far from relieving them of their academic burden, increases the burden as they must now answer to a tutor in addition to the course professor.

Finally, students who are at risk are notorious for their reluctance to refer themselves for assistance until much too late. Whether through denial, pride, or ignorance, students who need help the most are least likely to request it. So goes the axiom of the learning assistance trade (Somers, 1988).

SI first developed in an institution that did not fit into the medical model described previously in this chapter. At UMKC, students can register as late as the first day of class, with their prior transcripts and test score data to be submitted sometime before the beginning of the following semester. This large, inner-city, commuter institution typically turned over 40 percent of its students each semester, most of them due to transfer but some due to the phenomenon now known as "stopping out" as distinguished from "dropping out." "Stopping out" refers to the widespread practice of taking no classes during a semester that would be devoted to other priorities, such as working to reestablish a bankroll sufficient to allow subsequent reentry.

Delivery of services from the first day of class changes the support program from a *reactive* to a *proactive* mode. One of the noncognitive variables that differentiates between more capable and less capable students is this: those who are less capable are inclined to do without support services until they need them; those who are more capable will avail themselves of services at the beginning and stop services if they find the services to be neither productive nor essential. The presence of these more capable students in support sessions affirms that the sessions are not remedial. That fact enables less capable students to participate without the fear of stigma.

The integration of skills and content allows the SI leader to meet the perceived content needs of students while delivering essential skills instruction simultaneously. If, as McLuhan argued, "the medium is the message," then the message of SI is skill instruction, delivered along with the course content material.

Delivering services on an outreach basis, that is, in the classroom buildings assigned for regular academic instruction, lends an air of academic credibility to the support service. Similarly, the overt endorsement of the SI program from the participating course professor lends further authority to the claim that SI is valuable.

Of course, the voluntary nature of the SI pact which is renewable every week (or every day, for that matter) comforts the wary student who shuns taking on additional responsibility. The combination of voluntary participation, early intervention, and proactive support differentiates the SI model from the traditional medical model that relies on diagnosis of signs and symptoms followed by prescriptive treatment.

Conclusion

It has been nearly two decades since Supplemental Instruction first appeared in higher education. After starting at the University of Missouri–Kansas City in 1973, SI has been implemented at a variety of institutions across the United States and around the world. Borrowing ideas from developmental psychology, SI has attempted to encourage students to become actively involved in their own learning. By integrating appropriate study skills with the review of the course content, students begin to understand how to use the learning strategies they have heard about from teachers and advisors. As new educational theories and practices have surfaced, the SI model has been adapted to incorporate the best in educational research.

With the increasing diversity of today's college students and the advent of alternative admission programs, the student body is continuing its evolution into a heterogeneous group reflective of American society. The popular and professional literature often carries articles decrying the poor academic preparation level of students or the poor quality of teaching by classroom professors. Few solutions have been offered that work. From our point of view, the matter is moot. Many professors have tenure and colleges need all the students that they can recruit. Rather than blaming either party, strategies must be developed that allow students to succeed while ensuring that academic standards are maintained, if not strengthened. SI, as one component, can contribute to an overall institutional plan for student success.

References

Blanc, R. A., DeBuhr, L., and Martin, D. C. "Breaking the Attrition Cycle: The Effects of Supplemental Instruction on Undergraduate Performance and Attrition." *Journal of Higher Education*, 1983, *54* (1), 80–89.

Bridgham, R. G., and Scarborough, S. "Effects of Supplemental Instruction in Selected Medical School Science Courses." *Academic Medicine RIME Supplement*, 1992, *67* (10), 569–571.

Christie, N. G., and Dinham, S. M. "Institutional and External Influences on Social Integration in the Freshman Year." *Journal of Higher Education*, 1991, *62*, 412–436.

Dimon, M. "Why Adjunct Courses Work." *Journal of College Reading and Learning*, 1988, *21*, 33–40.

Keimig, R. T. *Raising Academic Standards: A Guide to Learning Improvement*. ASHE-ERIC Higher Education Report, no. 4, Washington, D.C.: Association for the Study of Higher Education, 1983. (ED 233 669)

Martin, D. C., and Arendale, D. (eds.). *Supplemental Instruction: Improving First-Year Student Success in High-Risk Courses*. Columbia, S.C.: National Resource Center for the Freshman Year Experience, 1992.

Martin, D. C., and Arendale, D. "Supplemental Instruction: Improving Student Performance, Increasing Student Persistence," 1990. (ED 327 103)

Martin, D. C., and Gravina, M. "Serving Students Where They Fail: In Class." *Thresholds of Education*, Aug. 1990, *26*, 28–30.

Martin, D. C., Blanc, R. A., DeBuhr, L., Alderman, H., Garland, M., and Lewis, C. *Supplemental Instruction: A Model for Student Academic Support*. Kansas City, Mo.: University of Missouri and ACT National Center for the Advancement of Educational Practices, 1983.

Martin, D. C., and Blanc, R. A. "The Learning Center's Role in Retention: Integrating Student Support Services with Departmental Instruction." *Journal of Developmental Education*, 1981, *4*, 2–4, 21–23.

Martin, D. C. "Learning Centers in Professional Schools." K. V. Lauridsen (ed.), *New Directions for College Learning Assistance: Examining the Scope of Learning Centers*. San Francisco: Jossey-Bass, 1980.

Martin, D. C., Lorton, M., Blanc, R. A., and Evans, C. *The Learning Center: A Comprehensive Model for College and Universities*. Kansas City, Mo.: University of Missouri, 1977. (ED 162 294)

Maxwell, M. "Does Tutoring Help? A Look at the Literature." *Review of Research in Developmental Education*, 1990, *7* (4), 1–5.

Noel, L., Levitz, R., and Saluri, D. (eds.). *Increasing Student Retention: Effective Programs and Practices for Reducing the Dropout Rate.* San Francisco: Jossey-Bass, 1985.

Somers, R. L. *Causes of Marginal Performance by Developmental Students.* Boone, N.C.: National Center for Developmental Education, Appalachian State University, 1988.

Stahl, N. A., Simpson, M. L., and Hayes, C. G. "Ten Recommendations from Research for Teaching High-Risk College Students." *Journal of Developmental Education,* 1992, *16* (1), 2–4, 6, 8, 10.

Tinto, V. *Leaving College: Rethinking the Causes and Cures of Student Attrition.* Chicago: University of Chicago Press, 1987.

DAVID R. ARENDALE is national project director for Supplemental Instruction and associate director of the Center for Academic Development at the University of Missouri–Kansas City.

An increasing number of students need developmental help.
Supplemental Instruction can raise the level of success dramatically.

Steps in Starting
Supplemental Instruction

Len Ainsworth, Don Garnett, DaNay Phelps,
Scott Shannon, Ken Ripperger-Suhler

Supplemental Instruction (SI) is subject related. Historically, SI stems from faculty after-class help, how-to-study sessions, tutor assistance, and peer discussions of concepts and procedures. SI formalizes the process and adds a unique dimension.

A number of studies document the effectiveness of SI, which combines content review with study strategy training, in varied settings and for diverse sets of students. SI has been found effective in math and math-based courses (Allen, 1993; Kenney, 1989; Phelps and Ripperger-Suhler, 1992). Martin and Arendale (1992) documented benefits for students regardless of entrance exam scores and previous academic success. These findings strengthen the idea that SI is an appropriate means to reach institutional goals for the development of first-year college students (Upcraft and Gardner, 1989). This chapter describes a how-to-start scenario using math as the subject example.

Student Needs and the Challenge for
Supplemental Instruction

Instructors in traditional entry-level math classes must work with many students who lack effective study habits, skills, or both for learning in the college instructional environment. Teachers in developmental math classes must confront skill weaknesses, as well as defeatist attitudes, among the students needing their assistance. First-year students and returning students alike often view themselves as "non-math" persons, unable to master computational requirements of college math.

Mathematics' vocabulary, reading skills, critical-thinking abilities, and problem-solving techniques represent major needs of developmental students, especially those whose competence level is below College Algebra. Mathematics "involves clarification of the problem, deduction of consequences, formulation of alternatives and development of appropriate tools" (Committee on the Mathematical Sciences in the Year 2000, National Research Council, 1989, p. 5). Students who lack skills are not likely to become successful in a lecture course in mathematics. Students' inability to function as "independent learners" puts them at risk of continuing their high school patterns of low achievement or failure. While assessment and developmental advising can help place students in appropriate courses, Supplemental Instruction should be considered as a potential intervention strategy.

Dweck and Licht (1980, p. 198) differentiate between students who are helpless and those who have a "mastery orientation." This distinction is closely related to the dependent/independent categorization applied to students newly arrived on college campuses. Because SI affirmatively and demonstrably addresses the relationship between student effort and success, it can be considered a form of "attributional retraining" (Perry and Penner, 1990). As such, it can be useful to students with histories of personal failure, as well as those who simply lack the skills for "doing math."

While the activities of independent learning are intuitive for some students, training aimed at student development formalizes the process. The SI paradigm partially meets the challenge of developing a structured process. For example, SI encourages students to develop problem-solving strategies (Allen, Kopas, and Stathis, 1993). The literature on human helplessness and intellectual achievement helps clarify why the SI approach is conducive to the development of independent learners. The remainder of the essay will clarify an example of initiating SI.

Getting Started

SI shows promise in a variety of educational settings. The administration, among others, can communicate the promise of SI to the various echelons of the institution. SI will likely get a warm reception if administrators and faculty see some potential help in increasing math competencies and, thereby, enhancing retention.

Faculty need to know what SI proposes to do. Administrators want to know if they can afford SI programs. Learners need convincing that their competencies can be improved.

Research is the first step for obtaining institutional support. The university or college, depending on the academic structure, can forge alliances of the college or university to conduct research among the first college mathematics courses. For example, directors of freshman studies programs, institutional research, undergraduate mathematics faculty, and personnel in learning centers can join forces to discover the trends of mathematics enrollment and retention rates from the freshman to sophomore years. If SI can establish correlations between unacceptable attrition rates and initial low-enrollment success in mathematics, the administration and faculty will likely respond. Presidents, vice presidents, deans of instruction, retention committees, faculty committees, even governing boards, and other decision-making groups on campus will be interested in hard data that reveal a problem, particularly if that data proposes possible solutions.

Relating your research to current realities should be step two. Increasingly, state departments of higher education and state legislatures are calling for accountability and are even beginning to tie funding to graduation rates of particular programs. The implication of these legislative actions aimed at reducing states' costs for higher education, combined with documented needs for SI on campus, may secure the support needed to begin or extend an SI program in mathematics.

SI structure needs broad-based participation. Unless faculty and administrators "buy in" to the SI program, it will not achieve its potential to improve the success of first college mathematics courses.

Once SI achieves administrative and faculty support and a budget, a Supplemental Instruction Advisory Committee should be established. Let us assume that SI will be new to campus with mathematics as a primary focus. Learning center personnel, advising center representatives, faculty, and administrators should be part of the advisory committee providing continued monitoring and support.

If the institution's enrollment warrants, the SI supervisor should be full time. If this is not possible, the university needs to clearly define the responsibilities as part of the person's job description and train that individual in SI supervision and communication of the program goals to SI leaders, faculty, and administrators. The supervisor will be responsible for program evaluation, modification, and research to document the success of the program. Furthermore, the supervisor should be prepared to explain and promote the program to the Advisory Committee, the Board of Regents, and the media. The ability to select, train, supervise, and evaluate students is critical. A supervisor could come from the discipline faculty or the Student Affairs division as long as this individual meets the qualifications listed above. Ideally, the supervisor should be a developmental educator who understands the psychology of the "at-risk" learner.

Selection of SI leaders is important for the long-range success of the program. For example, in developmental mathematics courses, the best SI leaders may be those who have earned an "A" or "B" in the targeted course and then gone on to achieve similar grades in higher-level math classes. Students meeting these criteria can serve as a primary pool of applicants for SI leaders. If such students are in short supply, individuals with a history of tutoring can be an excellent second source of SI leaders. All leaders selected for the program should be warm, outgoing, and empathic. It is helpful if they derive pleasure from watching students progress, but they must be able to place responsibility for the progress on the student. Other selection criteria include the ability to work with peers and accept instruction and advice from others involved in the administration of SI. Some other sources of SI leaders merit discussion. For example, if an institution has a strong teacher education program, upper division mathematics and business education majors who are training to be teachers may be particularly effective in math SI. However, other mathematics majors should not be ignored. All SI leaders should be carefully selected on the basis of the entire list of leader characteristics.

Those selected should complete formal training under the direction of the supervisor. Even if regular teaching assistant (TA) training programs exist on campus, the institution needs SI training. In addition to the standard aspects of SI training, leaders will need additional direction in the use of placement tests, verbal protocols, student-developed glossaries, leader responses to requests for "the answers," and in the process of using the SI session routine to develop student learning independence.

Recruiting students into the SI sections can be challenging, as students may initially view SI as extra work. Visor, Johnson, and Cole (1992) provide several recommendations which include: "hosting faculty members" who enthusiastically support the program during class, academic advisors, counselors-as-advocates who refer students to the program, and SI personnel who make presentations during the lecture segment of the class regarding effectiveness of SI. A combination of these approaches may be time-intensive, but will prove preferable to coercion, such as grade penalties or rewards. One SI leader reported a negative influence from unmotivated students who refused to participate but came to SI because their instructor required SI session attendance in the course grading scheme.

Evaluation and research goals should be part of the initial design of every SI program in mathematics. Evaluation under the direction of the supervisor must be ongoing. Every program should be unique to the institution, the result of clearly established objectives and modifications that result from evaluation.

Just because a program has worked on one campus does not mean that it will work on another. However, with adaptations based on the institution's particular needs, each campus can have an effective SI program in math. Students, leaders, and the supervisor should all evaluate the SI sessions at the end of the semester. In addition, your evaluation research plan should include a longitudinal study of the students who achieve success in a developmental math course and the next required course or courses. Continued administrative support for the SI program will be easier if one can document the success of the students SI assists.

Session Goals and Approach

According to Resnich and Ford (1991, p. 249), "learners do not simply add new knowledge. Instead, they must convert the new information to already established knowledge structures and construct new relationships among those structures." SI, using verbal protocols, can encourage students to construct new relationships in math.

SI leaders teaching the process of protocols may expect to encounter resistance if students perceive SI requires them to do extra work, especially if they suspect that it is "busy work." SI leaders should introduce protocols gradually, modeling them with simple content and initially providing complete examples. A typical problem-solving process can encourage students to develop problem-solving skills both at the general and content specific levels. The steps are:

1. *List* what you know about the work problem.
2. Determine what you are *trying to find out*.
3. Describe in words the *relationship* between what you know and what you want to find out.
4. Describe the relationship between what you know and what you want to find out using, for example, a *mathematical expression*.
5. *Solve* the mathematical expression.

The leader can walk the students through the use of the protocol in a group setting. If students can experience success while using protocols in the group, they may accept increased responsibility for producing the documents on their own. Students should be weaned gradually from the complete protocol to one with blanks to full responsibility for producing the entire document. The value of students completing such protocols may extend beyond the collection of documents on mathematics problem-solving. With direction, students may learn to develop problem-solving protocols for other classes and may even acquire a more internal locus of control.

A glossary can provide the student with a sense of accomplishment that builds the confidence needed to overcome periods of discouragement. Glossaries consist of key terminology, student-developed definitions, examples, and illustrations. SI leaders can reinforce glossary development and use results in improved performance on exams and homework, both tangible results that can be reinforced by SI leaders. The goal is to have students come to the SI sessions with their glossaries prepared and be willing to share the work with the SI group. Consistent use of glossaries and protocols should lead to continued gradual growth, which is critical for students attempting to learn to persist in situations that have previously caused them to quit or fail. First-year students with such backgrounds are especially likely to withdraw from or quit performing in a math course when it becomes difficult. Hence, we urge that instruction include "modeling mathematical ideas through the use of representations (concrete, visual, graphical, symbolic)" in accord with current standards for math teaching (Commission, 1989, p. 151) as well as the explicit teaching of problem-solving techniques in courses with high student failure and withdrawal rates. SI is uniquely structured to provide this type of learning experience for mathematics.

Conclusion

Several points are considered critical in the development of an effective SI program. Administratively, the implementing department should ensure the execution and evaluated outcome of each of the following steps: determining the need, selecting the target courses, establishing institutional support, selecting (and training) an SI supervisor, selecting (and training) SI leaders, developing instructional approaches, recruiting students, documenting results, and using evaluation for improvement.

While SI sessions may vary somewhat in the focus of responsibility (teacher- or student-centered), students must experience the sessions as providing real benefits in a warm and encouraging environment if they are to continue to actively participate. Facilitators must require students to accept a significant level of responsibility for developing skills that they can use to become independent learners. SI for mathematics courses may help more students (especially marginal students) if the sessions are more structured than the traditional SI model. The structure should facilitate the development of vocabulary and problem-solving skills, and foster the willingness to persist purposefully in the face of failure. Studies show that students who develop these skills possess some level of mastery orientation toward their mathematics courses.

References

Allen, M., Kopas, S., and Stathis, P. "Supplemental Instruction in Calculus I at Glendale Community College." *SI News,* Spring 1993, *1,* p. 3.

Commission on Standards for School Mathematics of the National Council of Teachers of Mathematics. *Curriculum and Evolution of Standards for School Mathematics,* Reston, Va.: National Council of Teachers of Mathematics, 1989.

Committee on the Mathematical Sciences in the Year 2000, National Research Council. *Everybody Counts: A Report to the Nation on the Future of Mathematics Education.* Washington, D.C.: National Academy of Research, 1989.

Dweck, C. S., and Licht, B. "Learned Helplessness and Intellectual Achievement." M. Seligman and J. Garber (eds.), *Human Helplessness: Theory and Applications.* New York: Academic Press, 1980.

Kenney, P. A. "Effects of Supplemental Instruction on Student Performance in a College Level Mathematics Course." Presented at the annual meeting of the American Educational Research Association, San Francisco, Mar. 1989.

Martin, D. C., Arendale, D. (eds.). *Supplemental Instruction: Improving First-Year Student Success in High-Risk Courses.* Columbia, S.C.: National Resource Center for the Freshman Year Experience, 1992.

Perry, R. P., and Penner, K. S. "Enhancing Academic Achievement in College Students Through Attributional Retraining and Instruction." *Journal of Educational Psychology,* 1990, *82,* 262–271.

Phelps, D., and Ripperger-Suhler, K. "The Use of SI in Math 0302 at Texas Tech University." Report to the Office of Supplemental Instruction, University of Missouri–Kansas City, 1992.

Resnich, L. B., and Ford, W. W. *The Psychology of Mathematics Instruction.* Hillsdale, N.J.: Lawrence Erlbaum, 1991.

Upcraft, M. L., Garner, J. N. (eds.). *The Freshman Year Experience: Helping Students Survive and Succeed in College.* San Francisco: Jossey-Bass, 1989.

Visor, J. N., Johnson, J. J., and Cole, L. N. "The Relationship of Supplemental Instruction to Affect." *Journal of Developmental Education,* 1992, *16* (2), 12–18.

LEN AINSWORTH *is professor of education and vice provost at Texas Tech University, Lubbock.*

DON GARNETT *is director of the University Transition Advisement Center at Texas Tech University.*

DANAY PHELPS *is advising coordinator for the University Transition Advisement Center at Texas Tech University.*

SCOTT SHANNON *is instructor in the Department of Mathematics at South Plains College in Levelland, Texas.*

KEN RIPPERGER-SUHLER *is a graduate student in sociology at Texas Tech University.*

Supplemental Instruction can help all of us—including administrators and faculty—become active learners. Here is how Supplemental Instruction contributed to one college's faculty development plan.

Faculty Development Through Supplemental Instruction

Sherrin Marshall

Through funds provided by the Fund for the Improvement of Postsecondary Education (FIPSE), Salem State College was able to use a well-established student academic assistance program, known as Supplemental Instruction (SI), to foster student academic development. While the primary focus of SI is on improved academic achievement by students, it can also be beneficial for faculty members. Therefore, Salem State College simultaneously employed SI as a vehicle for the professional development of faculty. As time passed, it was used as a means to encourage qualities of student leadership and stimulate interest in teaching as a career as well.

The SI program sets up a regular schedule of out-of-class sessions in which groups of students work together to master course content. These sessions provide an informal, nonthreatening setting for students to review the material, use the language of the discipline, organize their notes, and prepare for exams. The results are that students improve both academic skills and understanding of the course content. Within this informal environment, students interact with the subject content, while other students often provide models of successful study strategies. Thus, content deficits as well as student skill deficits are addressed.

At the outset of the grant in the mid 1980s, faculty at Salem State, like their counterparts at similar institutions, had little awareness of how to effectively address the needs of underprepared learners. The typical faculty participant, a full professor who had been at Salem State for more than fifteen years, often felt that attempts to address skill deficiencies in students were really directed at him or her. In other words, many faculty felt unspoken accusations of helping students to fail. Additionally, many faculty members believed that they were not being encouraged to maintain high standards, and they concluded that lowering standards was the only means by which students would demonstrate improved performance. As a result, when the SI program began, faculty were often resentful and even vociferously defensive of their teaching methods and choice of course content.

Many faculty had become burned out or frustrated by their experiences of teaching "high-risk courses" or courses in which thirty percent or more of the students receive a D, F, or W at the semester's end. Although high-risk classes sometimes fall outside a student's career interests, passing them is often mandatory for access into or for continuation within particular majors or fields of study. Students attend these classes because they "have to be there," and many do not have the internal motivation to achieve in these subjects, much less excel. The courses selected for the program were those that were the most high-risk as well as those that served the largest numbers of students. So, from the beginning, we focused our assistance toward the "high-risk course" rather than toward the "high-risk student."

The typical Salem State student attended a large urban high school and may have encountered only true-false or multiple choice exams due to the large class sizes that make grading large numbers of essay exams infeasible. Such students, especially less experienced freshmen and sophomores, often panic when they encounter college courses in which they must pass essay exams that demand the skillful use of analytical forms of writing and critical thinking. All too often, students may never have been required to think or write analytically. Failure on the first test of their college level skills and abilities can be demoralizing to students. Concomitantly, faculty also frequently became unmotivated and alienated in and through their experiences with underprepared students. In other words, faculty did not enjoy teaching these courses any more than students enjoyed taking them.

A Typical Scenario

Although interviews with several hundred students in academic difficulty at Salem State and informal talks with many faculty members led to the conclusions presented in the preceding paragraphs, the real impetus for a Supplemental Instruction program arose from my experiences with two individuals. One student, a freshman named Jose C., came to see me at the beginning of his second semester at Salem State in the spring of 1985. Because he was on academic probation, the college required that he meet with me in my capacity as director of academic advising. Some of Jose's problems were typical of the probationary student. Jose was the eldest of eight children, the first in his family to attend college, and worked off-campus almost thirty hours a week. His father, opposed to the idea of Jose attending college, thought he should quit and work full time.

Thus far, this was an all-too-familiar story. But other aspects about Jose were atypical. When I reviewed his Strong-Campbell Interest Inventory Test with him, I noticed immediately that his academic comfort score of 67 was uncommonly high for probationary students at Salem State, who often presented scores of six to ten. Jose's score was in fact among the highest I had seen at Salem State. It seemed that Jose was highly motivated to achieve academically and, in fact, persuaded me in the course of our interview that he intensely desired to remain in school. Even though English was not his first language, Jose enrolled in eighteen credit hours in an attempt to recoup the credits he had lost through his first semester's poor performance. All these factors attest to his high motivation; Jose, unlike the typical probationary student, had no motivational deficits.

One of Jose's greatest problems was with the required science sequence. He had enrolled in the second semester of biology, although he had only earned a grade of D for the previous semester. Now he was working hard, but was clearly in over his head. If he were to have any chance of succeeding, Jose would need extensive academic support. When I telephoned his biology professor, Dr. S., to see if extra help was available for Jose, the professor vented his frustrations.

"What am I supposed to do with students like that?" he asked angrily. "That student needs more help than I can possibly give him during my office hours. We admit too many like him. I'm just trying to maintain academic standards at this place, and no one appreciates that. Why don't you talk to the vice president about our admissions policies, instead of talking to me?"

In my capacity as retention officer at Salem State, I kept the records on student attrition for the Office of Academic Affairs and conducted exit interviews with many, if not most, of the students who withdrew. Jose became another statistic when he withdrew in the middle of the semester; he simply stopped attending, in part, I suspect, to avoid having to talk with me. Dr. S., his professor, became a statistic of a different sort; he took early retirement the following year.

What was I to do? Instead of counting students like Jose as attrition statistics, I wanted to help them succeed. Neither could I see Dr. S. as the villain of this scenario. He typically lectured to nearly one hundred students of very diverse backgrounds and abilities in each section of his introductory course. Dr. S., who usually taught two and sometimes three of these sections, had no real idea how to teach them more effectively. He was tired, alienated, and felt blamed for the failure of students such as Jose.

Pilot Program and FIPSE Funding

Realizing that help was essential for both students and faculty, I believed the college could use Supplemental Instruction to address the issues and concerns of both groups in meaningful and constructive ways. The previous year I had been impressed with a presentation Deanna Martin had given on a Supplemental Instruction (SI) program she had developed. I saw SI as a possible vehicle to bring much needed help to both students and faculty. Could a solid, content-based academic assistance program that helped students grasp "how to learn" within the context of a particular course also aid faculty in learning about "how to teach?" I thought it was possible; however, I was already working hard in my capacity as director of academic advising. Although I had developed a program whereby faculty volunteers came in to assist me a few hours a week in the Academic Advising Center, I had no part- or full-time professional help, and no funds were available to mount an unproven program.

Fortunately, the academic vice president for academic affairs, William Mahaney, was willing to give my ideas a try since he too recognized the problems. In the fall of 1985, we began with a pilot program of three faculty members from the accounting, history, and English departments and hired three SI leaders to work with them. Mahaney encouraged me to develop a FIPSE grant proposal and promised that upon receipt of that grant, matching funds would be found to keep the program. From the outset, we believed this assistance would not only aid students in learning more effectively but also assist faculty in teaching more effectively. We believed that the SI program could help both learners and faculty additionally discover or rediscover the joy within their respective courses and disciplines.

The success of the 1985 pilot program was clear when the students who attended SI sessions performed better and completed their courses successfully more often, sometimes considerably more often than their peers. We submitted statistics on the program's initial success in our final proposal to FIPSE in Spring 1986. With the FIPSE award, we were able to expand and rigorously test the program. A total of twenty-four different faculty took part in the program over the time period of the pilot and three-year FIPSE grant. In Year One, 1986–87, we had five faculty and five SI leaders. In Year Two, the number rose to nine each, and in Year Three, fifteen faculty and fifteen SI leaders were involved.

The year following the grant's expiration, 1989–90, nineteen faculty participated with nineteen SI leaders. The program still continues at this writing despite changes in the administration and project director. In 1989, two faculty participants directed the project; in 1990, despite the state of great fiscal exigency, the college expanded the program. Of those faculty who did not continue, one retired, one became a department chair, and one dropped from the program because he failed to honor his commitment to attend monthly seminars.

Building Support for Supplemental Instruction

With the support of the academic vice president and the department chairs, I concentrated my efforts on soliciting participation from among the most dispirited faculty members. The typical faculty participant was a full professor who had taught at Salem State for more than fifteen years. Since the majority of faculty members at Salem State had no experience with academic assistance programs other than tutorials, which we judged to be less effective in addressing the needs of these high risk courses, I first talked with each professor individually. I provided faculty participants with literature on SI, responded to their questions, and suggested they try the program for one year. If they failed to see results, particularly in terms of improved learner outcomes, they would not be obligated to continue. This proved to be the means by which we "sold" them the program.

Participation was wholly voluntary, and an overwhelming majority of faculty approached were willing to try the program. However, not all faculty were interested. One individual called me "a lackey and spy for the administration." Another stated that this was a "remedial program for remedial faculty" that could only improve student academic performance by forcing professors to lower their standards. Hence, she had no interest in participating. The program flourished despite these pockets of resistance.

Faculty Involvement with Training

In our project, faculty were encouraged to participate in interviewing and selecting SI leaders; most did so. Faculty nominated students who had successfully completed these high-risk courses. The project director gave faculty and SI leaders an overview of the group approach that SI employs and the ways it differs from more traditional individualized tutoring approaches. Selection and training of SI leaders also provided a means to familiarize faculty with the program. Additionally, the project required that all faculty participate in training newly appointed SI leaders and present a mock lecture or help run a mock SI session. Professors were also drawn into the discussions of the benefits, to students and faculty alike, of having "active" learners instead of "passive" learners in the classroom. In retrospect, this was a critical first step toward faculty ownership of the program. We regarded faculty as colleagues working with us as integral team members on aspects crucial to the program's success.

At Salem, we encouraged faculty to work directly with their SI leaders by meeting with them once each week to set goals and review progress, although faculty never knew the names of students who were actually attending SI sessions until after the term's end. After the program's first year, the faculty and SI leaders expanded this activity, since many faculty found feedback from SI leaders extremely valuable. Just as they came to trust the program as a source of help, they came to trust their SI leaders. This helped foster an atmosphere of collegiality and trust that made critical self-assessment on the part of the individual faculty possible.

Seminar Component

One essential aspect of our project consisted of monthly meetings or seminars. Some were for faculty alone, some for SI leaders only, and some brought both groups together. Faculty suggested topics of interest and concern, while the project director actually planned and directed the seminars in which the entire group participated. Faculty requested some repeat seminars; others arose from questions raised earlier. Each illuminated problems and issues related to teaching and learning. Utilizing a collaborative approach, the format of the seminars encouraged collegiality.

Since SI's inception, faculty seminars included:

1. A colloquium and discussion presented by Salem State's psychology department on "Understanding Motivation," which highlighted psychological research on the subject of motivation and offered specific ways by which faculty could assist students in becoming more motivated to learn.
2. Strategies for teaching large compared with small groups of students.
3. "Show-and-tell" teaching strategies in which faculty planned and presented their trade secrets with great enthusiasm.
   The format included:
   a. One good idea that worked for me in my lectures.
   b. One good idea that didn't work.
   c. One bad idea from which I still learned.
4. Videotaping and critiquing of faculty teaching performance where faculty presented three-minute presentations to their peers. Faculty who felt they had specific problems were able to work voluntarily with the project director on an individual basis.
5. A colloquium and discussion on using SI in introductory calculus and physics courses.
6. Troubleshooting and problem solving.
7. A colloquium and discussion on "Dealing with Issues of Racism and Sexism in the Classroom."

Joint meetings included:

1. Analyzing and evaluating our statistical data from each semester. This served a number of purposes since we were able to give faculty members the feeling that improving student performance was laudable but not meant to be competitive.
2. Designing, editing, and critiquing a videotape made to publicize our program.
3. Assessing each year at its close and planning the next.
4. Assessing and evaluating the training of new SI leaders and additions to training.

A series of monthly seminars for faculty and student SI leaders developed, using a practical more than theoretical approach. The format of these seminars allowed discussion time for sharing of ideas and reactions. We selected the seminar topics for in-depth exploration of various issues related to teaching and learning. Implicit in the $1,000 remuneration the faculty received each year for their participation was the assumption that they live up to the program's minimum expectations, which included the following:

1. Attendance at the training sessions of SI leaders.
2. Attendance at the monthly seminars.
3. Regular meetings with the SI leader in their courses.
(One faculty member attended only the training and none of the seminars. He was dropped from the program at the end of the semester.)

For some, the initial incentive for their participation was undoubtedly the $1,000 they received. As the project progressed, it became clear that money was no longer the most important motivation. (In fact, one faculty member went out of his way to repeatedly mention that the stipend had made it possible for him to buy a word processor with which he began a separate scholarly study. He felt guilty about taking the money.) Faculty stated that they would support the project even if no stipend was provided. Indeed, after the grant expired, every faculty member opted to continue on a voluntary basis. Moreover, they assumed many tasks related to the project on their own and continue to do these tasks. In large measure, the faculty's willingness to invest their own time was due to the project's results, both tangible and intangible.

Project Results

The benefits of SI demonstrated repeatedly at numerous institutions were evident from the outset at Salem State and continued to manifest themselves over the three-year grant cycle. The average student who attended SI sessions earned higher grades, often considerably higher than the class average. Students who attended SI sessions withdrew far less frequently from high-risk courses than students who failed to attend.

More surprising, perhaps, was that a statistically significant number of classes taught by participating faculty no longer fell in the category of high-risk courses. Participating faculty felt they had been able to raise rather than lower their standards while this change was taking place. In part, this transformation occurred because meaningful academic assistance was available for students. We also found a change in faculty attitudes and behavior. This information came from three sources:

1. The statistics on learner outcomes.
2. A pre- and postparticipation questionnaire that the psychology department helped develop and administer.
3. Individual (voluntary) interviews of one-half to one hour with faculty at the end of the program.

All of these measures suggested that the benefits of opening new channels of communication was creating a new institutional ethos at Salem State. A new spirit of cooperation developed among administration, faculty, and students as a result of the SI program.

Faculty Responses to Supplemental Instruction Leaders

Several faculty members came to feel that having the SI leader in class was inspirational for them and regarded their SI leaders as colleagues. Excerpts from an interview with a faculty participant about the SI leader in his class suggest this sense of enthusiasm: "The SI leader I have this year really took off. . . . He (the SI leader) follows up (on my lectures) and answers questions (with the) semi-peer approach that I can't do. I am a faculty member, and therefore I'm on the other side of the divide. He's older, but they don't know that. (It) has been fun (having the SI leaders in class). . . . They keep me on my toes. Dennis and I play off of one another. The more students that came (to SI sessions), the better. And they flocked to it. I had . . . forty students in the class; I think as many as thirty-one attended the SI on one occasion!"

A second faculty member described a changed classroom ethos as accompanying SI in this excerpt from his interview: "Having the SI leader in my class has changed the whole atmosphere and made the course not only better for students, but more enjoyable for me. . . . I used to see students come in the door and their body language said, 'This is just a required course that I'm going to hate.' Now, the students have a more positive attitude and ask more questions. I've encouraged the SI leader to raise her hand and let me know, right in class, what students aren't understanding. Then, I go over it immediately. . . . I still can't say this is my favorite course, since I do prefer teaching upper level courses in my discipline, but it's become much more enjoyable."

For their part, then, SI leaders provided a vital affirming element for faculty; they had succeeded in these courses. Moreover, their experiences as SI leaders undoubtedly enlarged their appreciation of their former professors as well as encouraged their interest in teaching as a profession.

Perhaps the central goal of SI is helping students to become "active learners" who can take charge of their own learning and become engaged in the learning process. At Salem State College, we felt such "active learners" would also better understand the purpose and value of the core curriculum in developing these new experiences in learning. This proved to be so. In training SI leaders, faculty and potential SI leaders were encouraged to discuss these complex goals, as well as more pragmatic plans. Such discussions were among the more inspirational aspects of the program for all concerned.

Additionally, faculty were encouraged to reassess their teaching methods and styles in a number of ways, formally or informally. Most did, and became better teachers as a result. One measure of effective teaching is that of student performance. Although the students who attended SI sessions showed the most marked improvement, *all* students in the course tended to perform better than students had in previous years in the same course with the same instructor. This unanticipated boon from the SI process attests, perhaps, to a more positive classroom ethos. Finally, professors came to feel better about themselves and their teaching. They were no longer alone; they had allies with whom they could discuss their problems.

Faculty Growth as a Result of the Salem State Program

For faculty, involvement with the program had varying levels of impact. Some faculty felt that they changed a good deal. As one said, "It's been a very positive experience for me. . . . I had the chance to meet with my colleagues and realize my colleagues had exactly the same problems in the classroom that I did! You get to know people differently in the situation that we had in our group seminars. Some people were able to be more direct, more honest than they'd ever been. [For instance] they could [now] say, 'Indeed, I have problems in the classes that I'm teaching,' or 'There are certain classes that I struggle with.' Such statements brought a perspective to me that I had not had before. I'd never had this opportunity to sit and talk with my colleagues in this manner." By the end of the program, this instructor's course was no longer a high-risk course.

Other faculty members, reflecting on their experiences, refused to acknowledge that they had any problems or difficulties to begin with and ascribed the changes they experienced to other factors in the program. One faculty member put it this way: "I was not burned out. I was complacent. I was looking for something new and was ready for a change, ready for something that was more collegial and interdisciplinary. The benefit to me was from talking with my colleagues . . . and there were also the benefit and feedback from working with my SI leader. I also saw benefit to the students. This program allows for some student-centered activities. It filled a very clear need for our students. . . . If it makes educational sense, why not stay in it? So I will, as long as my schedule allows." This faculty member, too, had stopped teaching "high-risk courses."

When asked what he felt the program had done for him, one faculty member responded: "Good things. It allowed me to reacquaint myself with people I really hadn't seen for years. . . . We met to talk for more than three minutes at a time in the program, and I met new people, too. . . . The chance to talk with people in other departments is important. . . . [The program] is cross-departmental. It's academic. It's personal. It's perhaps academic in the fullest sense of the term. [It provides] a chance, especially in World Civilizations, to interact, (or to) really talk with people in other departments, especially Biology. In talking with the [biology and physics faculty participants] about the History of Science, I discovered that their perception of Newton's role was very different from mine and differed significantly from that of a physicist." Thus, the program also provided a channel of communication for building interdisciplinary perspectives among participating faculty at Salem State.

Conclusion

Not all the problems that students and faculty experienced disappeared. To have made that happen would have required radical restructuring of the college, which is perhaps not a bad idea but not within the realm of the project.

The goal of the project was to empower faculty to change their courses and provide meaningful academic assistance for students; that happened.

One important result that is impossible to gauge or quantify pertains to institutional atmosphere or ethos. For some faculty and many, many students at Salem State, life has changed for the better as a result of our program. Faculty have some meaningful help for the problems they face working with underprepared and unmotivated students. Students know real academic assistance is available for them, and many specifically register for courses that offer sections of Supplemental Instruction. The new dean of arts and sciences sponsored three seminars on issues related to teaching and learning. All this came about despite the state of great fiscal exigency. The project succeeded because diverse constituencies were drawn into working together. To the extent that it continues, this program will continue to succeed.

SHERRIN MARSHALL is now senior policy analyst with the U.S. Department of Education Office of Educational Research and Improvement.

Supplemental Instruction sessions in the humanities are most successful when they are based on a sound understanding of the epistemology and axiology of the discipline.

Supplemental Instruction in the Content Areas: Humanities

Sandra Zerger

Although the University of Missouri–Kansas City initially developed Supplemental Instruction (SI) for science courses in the professional schools, it has also been successful in other disciplines and in different institutional types (Martin and Arendale, 1992). As an SI supervisor at Bethel College in North Newton, Kansas, and a certified trainer for SI, I have had the opportunity to experience SI in a variety of settings.

Understanding the Humanities

Recently I attended a symposium on our campus entitled "The Arts, Culture, and Community." Since I was working on this chapter, I tried to put a lens on my observations that would help me see what was different about such a symposium sponsored by the Division of Humanities and Fine Arts rather than the Division of Natural Sciences or the Division of Social Sciences (the three divisions of our college). I was struck by the vocabulary: *ambiguity, uncertainty, intuition, insight, self-knowledge, truths, process, symbolic representation.* How different these words are from those one would hear in the other divisions: *reliability, verifiability, clarity, empirical evidence, correspondence with natural laws, research methods, graphic representation.* Clearly, the differences are deeper than vocabulary.

By use of contrast, we can arrive at a better understanding of what is unique to the study of humanities and thereby suggest strategies to master material. Bazerman (1981) provides an excellent framework for understanding the differences among three academic discourses: biology, sociology, and literary criticism. He concludes that the professional writing in each of the three is discipline-specific in the following areas: (1) prior knowledge, (2) audience expectations, and (3) the nature of claims or evidence.

In biology, for example, the phenomena to be discussed is well known prior to the writing of the essay (for example, the location of a certain protein on DNA). The prior knowledge is codified and embedded in the language itself. The Latin scientific name contains all kinds of information, such as the number and kinds of atoms that make up compounds, the number of cells contained in the organism, whether or not the organism has fins or feathers, and whether or not the cell contains a nucleus with membranes that enclose their DNA.

The biologist does not need to discuss most of the relevant literature except for claims and evidence immediately and specifically bearing on the single phenomena that is the subject of the essay. The audience of biology shares evidence-gathering techniques, so the methods sections are often very short. In fact, methods sections are not meant to be read unless the reader is trying to replicate the research; the methods section may tell how many drops of a specific substance were used or the name of the procedure the study used, but little else. The biologist must present data that correspond to nature. It is up to nature to persuade.

For the sociologist, a phenomenon must be established and shown to be consequential. Much time is spent explaining the operational definitions and explaining and defending the particular method(s) used to gather evidence. Since prior literature is unsettled and open to interpretation, reviews of literature are extensive. The members of the audience share no uniform framework, so they must be convinced not only of the validity of specific claims by the author but also of the authenticity of an author's larger framework.

In literary criticism, the phenomenon (for example, a poem) is known; but the purpose is to re-create the subjective poetic moment. The criticism of the poem is particularistic and codification is entirely personal. The literary audience is concerned with private experiences. The critic must appear to have greater insight into the poem than previous critics have had. The final acceptance or rejection of the critic's view will be subjective, based upon a preponderance of evidence but with each bit of evidence weighted according to the values of each reader.

Understanding the epistemology of the humanities may *be* the content in introductory humanities courses and may be the prerequisite skill necessary to succeed in courses in the humanities. Wilson Yates (1993) argues that we need all the possible ways of seeing, using all available lenses to see more clearly; one lens is the humanities. The way of seeing and knowing is different from other disciplines. According to Yates, the power of the perspective of the humanities is in the greater clarity and depth with which it sees into inner streams, thereby opening up foundational truths. Sensory perception is necessary, of course, but the ultimate truth may not be perceived except by intuition. In the humanities, aesthetic forms—such as metaphor, image, sound, dance, narrative—lead to understanding.

Notice that even the definition of the epistemology in the humanities involves the use of metaphor, an emphasis on process, uncertainty (truths), and *self*-knowledge or individual insight. Because the truths about human nature tend, in the humanities, to be seen in a particular way, knowledge itself may be best understood if the context is understood; the time, the geography, the political and social context, and the linguistic environment all influence the epistemology. By contrast, the scientific method is predicated on the assumption that truth is time- and context-independent. In outlining the axioms of the positivistic paradigm, Lincoln and Guba (1985, p. 37) say that for the scientist "reality is single, tangible, and fragmentable." This epistemology may differ significantly from that held by some in the humanities and may cause problems for those from a different field. For example, Sheila Tobias (1992) says that physicists are used to having levels of certainty and find it difficult to pick out what is important in a literature class. The physicists in her study had difficulty studying literature because they were unsure what was important or what they should learn first. They compared studying literature to being in the suburbs where every house looks pretty much like the others; in contrast, they compared the study of physics to being in a city where there are skyscrapers and a varied landscape. That is, knowledge in physics is arranged vertically (certain things must be learned before others); whereas knowledge in the study of literature is not so vertical (the order of the courses is not very important; the student can take American Literature before Chaucer).

Students new to the humanities may have trouble with the axiology as well. Like the physicists in the Tobias study who needed landmarks, so, too, do students new to the discipline. The students struggle with the fact that while there may be no one right answer, not just any answer will do. Several spellings of a word in Shakespearean texts exist, but not just any spelling will do. Absolutes are difficult to find in modern English as well:

Different correct spellings—*plow/plough, catalog/catalogue, traveled/travelled.*
Different correct pronunciations, as for *economics, pianist, flutist, either,* or *height.*
Changing grammatical patterns, such as the dropping of the plural marker for *their*, as in "Everyone took their books to the meeting."

Even the artist who occupies a central position in his own discipline may struggle with the issue of certainty and judgment. When asked what he thought would be valued in art in the next decades, Paul Soldner (1993) answered, "If we knew, we would be producing it." Professors in the humanities complain that students want certainty rather than enjoying the struggle with complexity; students are not comfortable with questioning or with ambiguities and lack a map or framework out of which to build judgments. Professors in the humanities feel that the best answer or the best work of art may be the one the professor has not thought of. They eschew cookbook answers, or Muzak, or paint-by-number, or paintings which look like photographs.

They engage in a perpetual struggle between too early a closure (dogma) and no closure (complete relativism). Neither extreme is desirable to the humanists. James Luther Adams (1976, p. 25) argues that we must avoid "two equally enervating attitudes—a diffused identity, an unintegrated congeries of self-identifications on the one hand, and a foreclosed self-identity on the other hand." Adams prefers what he calls a "dynamic structure." Perhaps, then, the special "skill" necessary to master courses in the humanities is to accept a structure that is not rigid.

The method of presentation most prevalent in the humanities is talk. Language is valued; a well-turned phrase is applauded. In fact, in humanities classes there may not be much information put on the blackboard, and in the textbooks there many be few illustrations or diagrams. Contrast this method of presentation with the drawing of diagrams in a chemistry or biology class; the working of problems in a math, statistics, or physics course; or the graphs, charts, illustrations, and diagrams in social science texts. This lack of visual presentation in the humanities may be disconcerting for those used to having it.

In addition, the word *research* is used differently in the humanities. The closest the humanities come to what the sciences would call research is in areas which cross disciplines, such as in composition or sociolinguistic research, which use scientific, quasi-scientific, or naturalistic research methods. In literature, religion, or philosophy scholarship, a close analysis of a text is essential; citing secondary sources is not always essential. Research in the humanities usually means library reading. Sometimes, literary and art critics and philosophers summarize what other *scholars* have said, but they do not cite other *researchers* merely to back up their own points.

According to Bazerman (1981), other claims or evidence may include: references to other works by the same author to illuminate by analogy or contrast and references to the author's state of mind at the moment of artistic creation by means of letters, journals, or speeches by the author.

As previously noted, the job of the literary critic (or art critic, philosopher, or theologian) is to persuade the reading audience that this particular writer understands the text better than others have. As one professor of literature said, the student should find out all that is out there and then write something different (Zerger, 1991).

Even within the division of the humanities, subdivisions occur. Some students who have done well in art, religion, or literature classes still may have trouble writing papers in their first philosophy classes. McCarthy and Fishman (1991) found that in philosophy *research* means making up your own examples not only for your own viewpoint but for other positions as well, a kind of "mind research." Philosophers make up examples, and they use them to explore or modify generalizations and theory. In fact, a single hypothetical example may serve for three or four pages of philosophic writing. Anyone conducting SI in a philosophy class could profit from studying McCarthy and Fishman's article (1991), which explores the ways of knowing in philosophy and the expectations for good writing in the discipline.

Challenges for Supplemental Instruction Leaders

The observations that follow are primarily based on my personal observations as the Supplemental Instruction supervisor at Bethel College, a selective, small, residential, church-affiliated liberal arts college. Bethel College has had SI since 1979 and has consistently shown results that are congruent with the national data (one-half to one letter grade difference in the course grade even if the SI group and the non-SI group were equal to begin with, controlling for high school GPA, high school rank, Bethel GPA, ACT/SAT scores). Typical courses to which SI is attached in the humanities at Bethel College include Religion and Human Identity, Introduction to Philosophy, Introduction to the Visual Arts, and various literature courses. In addition, my work as a certified trainer in Supplemental Instruction has allowed me to train others and implement programs on other campuses. My observations from this vantage point lead me to assert that SI in the humanities is not merely a local phenomenon.

The epistemological and axiological issues in the humanities pose special challenges to the SI leaders in facilitating SI sessions in the humanities. If, as Tobias (1992) and Tobias and Tomizuka (1992) say, the tendency for science professors is to simplify complex ideas and literature professors favor probing for complexity, then SI leaders must help students move beyond simple answers in the humanities. The leaders have to design sessions that encourage elaboration rather than reduction of information. Students must go beyond memorizing items or terms. They must cut through the vocabulary of the discipline to get to the main ideas instead of repeating or memorizing words or phrases. For example, the professor may spend a lecture or two defining basic concepts such as *symbol, romance, pragmatism,* or *religion.* Students must go beyond a simple definition, even if they can cite the definition the professor prefers, to elaborating on the parts of the definition that are most important and to finding examples of the definition and negative examples as well. In fact, in the humanities, one frequently finds passages or even entire essays that are extended definitions. How different this is from the sciences where, according to Tobias and Tomizuka (1992, p. 24), "once you master a term in sciences, there's little room for error. You will know exactly what it meant when a term is used. Your instructor will know exactly what is meant when you use it." Leaders also must help students distinguish supporting detail from more important information. For example, students in an SI session at Bethel College for a humanities class, Religion and Human Identity, recently were discussing Potok's *The Chosen.* The leader had difficulty getting the students to relate the concepts in the book to the concepts related in class. They continually asked questions such as, "What did Danny do that day?" instead of "What does it mean to affirm the Jewish heritage and adapt and become free from it?" That is not to say that questions about details are not important, because they are. In fact, most meet the challenge of getting students to incorporate illustrations given in lectures and discussions into their notes. Unlike some high school classes, the illustrations are not superfluous but are essential to a full understanding of the material. In SI, students must practice utilizing details in their elaboration of larger questions. It is these larger questions that instructors ask students to address on examinations or in written essays. A fill-in-the-blank or a simple one- or two-sentence answer is not sufficient to explicate the complexities of the issues these subjects demand.

SI leaders in the humanities must also deal with emotion-laden words and concepts. Words such as *myth*, *liberal*, or *creation*, may be flash points for some students, causing them to come to a premature closure on the topic or to dismiss the concept completely. Concepts confronted in the humanities deal with deeply held personal beliefs, and students may have difficulty accepting new ideas in these areas. They may not even realize that they have closed out the concept and are being dogmatic.

On the other hand, SI leaders may have difficulty facilitating SI because the humanities require students to take a particular point of view without being relativistic. In this sense, students are asked to write as experts even in beginning courses. They are told to take a stand (develop a clear thesis) and to back it up with evidence that may be supporting points of logic, judgment, facts, or parts of the text. In other words, they are to use some specific supporting claims even in reaction papers, going far beyond, "I like it," or "I feel good about this text." Beginning students may feel that they cannot write anything new about the text and, thereby, have trouble writing anything at all. Or, they may feel that they must argue just as the professor has, not realizing that the professor welcomes an opposing point of view which is clearly developed and that they can get an "A" without agreeing with the professor.

In-class Activities by Successful Students

Students can significantly improve their performance in humanities courses by taking good, thorough notes from lectures. Tobias and Tomizuka (1992, p. 23) state that although scientists have to be fluent in both verbal language and universal languages of symbols and mathematics, what is different about science is that "sometimes it may be more efficient to think in symbols than in words and to write down equations rather than sentences." Students who are used to taking notes in this fashion or who have not had to take notes in high school in order to do well may find the kind of note taking required in the humanities to be difficult at first. The best advice for beginning students is to take down everything; it always is easier to pare down the words later than to recreate them.

Good notes in the humanities may mean finding a system to indicate who is saying what in class. Often students need to learn to take notes on discussions. Students typically quit taking notes when the class breaks into a discussion or when someone asks a question. In fact, they need to record the flow of the discussion, including what was asked and how it was answered, even if the answer came from other students in the class. For example, students can indicate when student A (S_A) asks a question and what student B (S_B) responds and how Professor John Smith (JS) answers or how he asks a further question. Professors often rely on comments made in such exchanges and do not repeat the ideas in a lecture format if they come out in such a classroom exchange. Typically, students are not accustomed to learning from such exchanges nor being tested on them, so these exchanges are not in their notes, and students are frequently surprised when test questions based on these interactions appear. In fact, students may not even remember that such material was presented in class. SI leaders can help ensure that students value discussion. Leaders may even be able to point out that when Professor Smith leaves the lectern and his notes to sit informally on the table, very significant course material will still be presented. Students often overlook the less formal presentations of material.

Strategies in Supplemental Instruction Sessions

Organization of Content. Students need to learn to see the big picture. They need to integrate topics, find common elements or themes. Recently, in a humanities class at Bethel College, the professor facilitated the students' finding common elements across texts by helping them build a matrix for the material (Figure 5.1).

Although students were generally able to fill in details such as Black Elk saw geese, horses, and buffaloes or the Buddhist saw a lotus, they had difficulty relating the texts to the larger theme of common elements of religious experiences. In fact, often they did not have the title of the matrix in their notes. Students may not realize that material presented is organized implicitly

Figure 5.1. Accounts of Religious Experiences

Text	"problem"	vividness	symbols	physical effect	outcome
Black Elk Speaks					
Morte in God Struck Me Dead					
Buddhist's vision The Way of the White Clouds					
The Life of the Holy Mother Teresa					

)r's mind in a matrix. One common problem students have when
:sented in a matrix pattern is that information often is given in a
anner (all of *Black Elk* first) but is tested in a vertical manner
1e types of 'problems' found in the religious experiences in the
texts we studied.") If matrices are not given explicitly in class, the SI leader
needs to help students see that such an organization may be implicit in the
material being presented. Students in the SI sessions can formulate the matrices together and work on filling in the needed content and generate possible
examination questions.

Sometimes students fail to see how individual lectures fit into the larger
themes of the course. For example, in a course the professor addressed the
larger theme of modernity in an initial lecture. He then invited various colleagues to lecture on the impact of modernity in their disciplines. The relationship of these lectures to the larger issue was outlined in the syllabus, but
although the students were seniors, many missed the connection between the
individual lectures and the larger theme. In SI, students can practice looking
for and elaborating on common themes in the course.

Issues of Language. Because the content of the humanities is particular,
students must pay close attention to what is said, how it is said, and by whom.
Historical language may pose problems for students. For example, when students misunderstand Socratic dialogue, the language itself may be the initial
problem that leads to misunderstanding of the ideas. In such cases, what is
said is not necessarily obvious. Students may need special glossaries, dictio-
naries, and explanations of the language. In the sessions, SI leaders can help
acquaint students with these aids and can ask students to rephrase words into
modern language to check for understanding. Special nuances of the language,
the nature of the argument, the connotations of the words used also are important. A cursory acquaintance (recognition learning or a dictionary definition)
is not sufficient for students to succeed in courses in the humanities. Techniques that foster elaboration help overcome these problems. SI leaders can
ask students to point out key words and phrases in a passage, use the ReQuest
procedure (Manzo, 1969), or ask students to provide concrete examples of certain words or phrases.

In order to help students cut through the tough ideas and unique vocabulary of a discipline to the main ideas, instead of repeating and memorizing
words, students can be asked to rephrase, point out key words in a passage,
and give concrete examples. In addition, they can write paraphrases in the text
as they read and learn to ask repeatedly, "What does this mean?"

Because students must become proficient in the primary mode of presentation in the humanities—words—many of the SI sessions in the humanities must stress verbal abilities. The most common of these are note review,
vocabulary building exercises, and focused discussion sessions. Brookfield
(1990) has a chapter on "Preparing for Discussion" and one on "Facilitating
Discussions," both of which offer useful techniques for SI leaders, including
what to do with students who talk too much and those who are silent.

Two other techniques prove invaluable for SI sessions in the humanities: the Informal Quiz and the One-Minute Paper. Developed by Martin and Blanc (1977), the title "Informal Quiz" implies a testing tool; yet this quiz is not intended as a method of formally evaluating student work. The focus is on learning rather than grading. In general, the Informal Quiz is used to develop and reinforce comprehension, improve retention of information, stimulate interest in a subject area and promote student participation in the study session.

At the opening of some SI sessions, the SI leader will ask all the students present to use some scrap paper to record answers to several questions posed by the SI leader. The questions generally are designed to have multiple answers. The paper is not turned in or seen by other students. If the students do not know the answer, they are encouraged to write down the question. After a few minutes of questions, the SI leader asks if anyone has an answer to any of the questions. Often the weaker students volunteer early so that they can share answers to the questions they feel confident about. The activity, which can take just a few minutes, helps establish a mind-set for the SI session, since the questions and their answers help identify critical concepts from the course material.

The One-Minute Paper, developed by Patricia Cross, is an effective yet simple device (Light, 1990, p. 36). An adaptation of the one-minute paper for SI is as follows. At the end of a session, each student can write answers to the following questions: (1) What is the big point you learned in yesterday's (this week's) lecture(s)? (2) What is the main question you had answered today? Or (as an alternative question for the beginning of the session), What one question would you like to have answered today?

Writing in the Humanities. Writing itself can pose special challenges for students in the humanities. SI in the humanities is often attached to courses in which students are graded and tested by essay (either essay exams or papers) because the course material requires more than a recognition knowledge of the material.

When writing is extensive, the SI session must respond with appropriate help in order for students to succeed. Although the SI session is not the place for one-on-one help with individual writing problems, it is a place where ideas can be generated and where students can practice predicting and answering possible test questions. One way this works well is to create a question, then ask students to brainstorm all the ideas and facts they know about the question. Students can put similar ideas together and state which facts support the ideas. The group can then write the first sentence or two of the proposed essay. Individuals can be encouraged to finish the practice essay on their own, and the leader can offer to read them. With courses that require papers, the SI session can first generate a good thesis and then discuss possible supporting evidence and ways to organize that evidence. Often, students need help identifying ways to find evidence, types of good sources, including sources other than typical library sources (books or periodicals). When appropriate, the use of interviews, museum exhibits, performances, computer programs, or maps should be encouraged. Students may need help understanding the purposes and nature of assignments as well. Also, SI leaders should be prepared to delineate possible writing strategies for the assignment. Helpful strategies are given by Walvoord (1986) in *Helping Students Write Well: A Guide for Teachers in All Disciplines.*

Another difficult writing assignment is a comprehensive final examination that requires students to integrate various topics or understand underlying themes across lectures. Often professors lay out their philosophy for the entire course in the first lecture or two of the semester. Students may not take notes on what they see as just "beginning things," and, sure enough, those lectures will be the basis for an essay question on the first exam and again on the final exam. A technique that helps students integrate the underlying themes across lectures is to continually relate the content to the themes of the course. By the end of the semester, each student should be able to articulate the purpose(s) of the course.

Issues of Authority and Evidence. Students new to the discipline may not pay sufficient attention to the author of a statement. Professors frequently summarize various scholars' positions ("according to Tillich"), but students may not write down the name of the scholar or critic; and then when asked to discuss a position that is identified by the scholar's name, they cannot do so.

Students need to become aware of how different scholars take different stands on the same issue. In my research, I found that beginning students often miss the different approaches to the same incident or text or fact. They tend to look at the common facts that appear in different sources rather than how these facts are used as evidence by the different authors (Zerger, 1991).

Visual Models. Because so many lectures in the humanities rely on words, SI sessions need to provide visual models. These visual models should help show how concepts are related to one another or offer alternate ways of understanding complex concepts. Venn diagrams, pictures, and matrices are all useful. Building such models together in the sessions helps students learn how to do these on their own. Figures 5.2 and 5.3 depict some representations that may suggest others.

Additional Strategies. Several additional general suggestions may help SI leaders. Brookfield (1990, p. 106) includes useful roles group members can take:

Recorder: makes a record of the group's deliberations
Summarizer: summarizes the group discussion at designated times—every fifteen minutes, for example
Detective: listens carefully and speaks out about the unacknowledged biases heard.

Establishing these roles or other appropriate roles allows SI groups to move beyond the expectation that the sessions will be dictated by the leader.

Figure 5.2. Symbols: Presentational and Representational

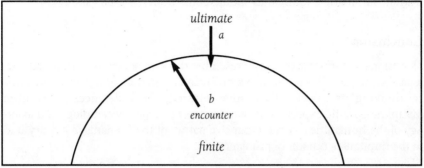

Types of Symbols: A presentational symbol makes the ultimate present in the finite realm (arrow a). A representational symbol allows those in the finite realm to encounter the ultimate (arrow b).

Figure 5.3. Sloan's Speaker-Audience Interaction

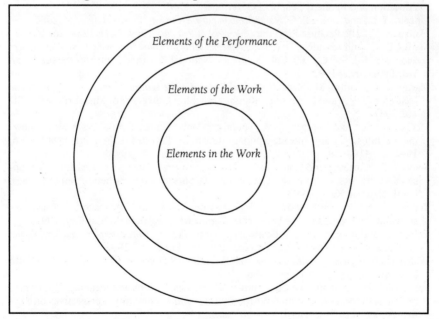

In fact, Brookfield (1990, p. 111) warns against the leader's laying down the truth in summaries; summaries should come from the group itself.

Conclusion

SI sessions in humanities clearly resemble those in social, physical, and biological sciences. They stress active involvement, participatory structure, critical thinking, and peer collaborative learning. The differences derive from discipline-specific expectations that have roots in the epistemology and axiology of the humanities, in the expansive nature of the humanistic inquiry, and in the humanist's pursuit of scholarship.

References

Adams, J. L. "The Purposes of 'Liberal' Education." In M. L. Stackhouse (ed.), *On Being Human Religiously: Selected Essays in Religion and Society.* Boston: Beacon, 1976.

Bazerman, C. "What Written Knowledge Does: Three Examples of Academic Discourse." *Philosophy of the Social Sciences,* 1981, *11,* 361–87.

Brookfield, S. D. *The Skillful Teacher.* San Francisco: Jossey-Bass, 1990.

Light, R. *Harvard Assessment Seminars: Explorations with Students and Faculty About Teaching, Learning, and Student Life.* Report No. 1. Cambridge, Mass.: Harvard Graduate School of Education and Kennedy School of Government, 1990.

Lincoln, Y. S., and Guba, E. G. *Naturalistic Inquiry.* Newbury Park, Calif.: Sage, 1985.

Manzo, A. V. "The ReQuest Procedure." *Journal of Reading,* 1969, 3 (2), 123–126, 163.

Martin, D. C., and Arendale, D. (eds). *Supplemental Instruction: Improving First-Year Student Success in High Risk Courses.* Columbia, S.C.: National Resource Center for the Freshman Year Experience, 1992.

Martin, D. C., Lorton, M., Blanc, R. A., and Evans, C. *The Learning Center: A Comprehensive Model for College and Universities.* Kansas City, Mo.: University of Missouri, 1977. (ED 162 294)

McCarthy, L. C., and Fishman, S. M. "Boundary Conversations: Conflicting Ways of Knowing in Philosophy and Interdisciplinary Research." *Research in the Teaching of English,* 1991, *25,* 419–468.

Soldner, P. "Curiosity and Courage: An Approach to Art." Paper presented at the Symposium on the Arts, Culture, and Community: Perspectives on Aesthetics. Bethel College, North Newton, Kans., 1993.

Tobias, S. "Professors as First-Year College Students: What Can They Teach Us?" Paper presented at the Freshman Year Experience Conference: Teaching, Kansas City, 1992.

Tobias, S., and Tomizuka, C. T. *Breaking the Science Barrier: How to Explore and Understand the Sciences.* New York: College Entrance Examination Board, 1992.

Walvoord, B. E. *Helping Students Write Well: A Guide for Teachers in All Disciplines.* New York: Modern Language Association, 1986.

Yates, W. "The Artist and the Community: Boundaries, Visions and Meaning." Paper presented at the Symposium on the Arts, Culture, and Community: Perspectives on Aesthetics, Bethel College, North Newton, Kans., 1993.

Zerger, S. "Literacy in College: The Use of Evidence in Reading and Writing of Undergraduates in Three Disciplines." Unpublished doctoral dissertation, Department of Curriculum and Instruction, University of Kansas, 1991.

SANDRA ZERGER is associate professor and director of the Center for Academic Development as well as certified trainer for Supplemental Instruction at Bethel College in North Newton, Kansas.

Look at the kinds of things that happen in specific Supplemental Instruction sessions and see how collaborative learning in mathematics takes place.

Supplemental Instruction Sessions in College Algebra and Calculus

Sandra L. Burmeister, Jeanne M. Carter,
Lynn R. Hockenberger, Patricia Ann Kenney,
Ann McLaren, Doris L. Nice

As SI supervisors who have experienced success using Supplemental Instruction (SI) in mathematics (Blanc, DeBuhr, and Martin, 1983; Martin and Arendale, 1992), we present our practical experiences and our examination of how SI works for students of mathematics. We hope that our colleagues who read this chapter will join our effort to continue defining SI's effectiveness and to test many ways of assisting students in mathematics.

The need for mathematics competency is clear. Mathematics is increasingly essential for modern careers and logical judgments. Yet, in some ways, mathematics is different from other disciplines. Many students come to the study of mathematics at the college level with great apprehension and anxiety. For such students, apprehension about mathematics or negative past experiences with mathematics may be due in part to the nature of the discipline itself. Success in mathematics requires daily practice and analysis, much like the repetitive work required to master a foreign language. If a student misses one concept in a lecture, the student may fail to understand 90 percent of what follows. Mathematics is an exacting discipline: to arrive at the correct answer, all steps must be accurate and performed in the right order. Correct solutions measure success in mathematics. Students often confuse this exactitude for rigidity of thought and assume that to excel in mathematics means to memorize recipes for solving problems. When students take tests in mathematics courses, exactness and even speed count. Furthermore, the vocabulary of mathematics is specialized and esoteric, much of it set aside exclusively for use in mathematics. Since students are not proficient in using mathematical terminology, they often use imprecise language instead of the correct terminology. Add to this the myth to which many students ascribe that only certain kinds of people can think mathematically. The active and collaborative learning that takes place during SI sessions, coupled with extensive solitary practice of mathematics, can make the discipline more accessible to all students who today must master mathematics.

We believe the SI model is one viable way of helping students succeed in mathematics courses because it is a carefully designed model. At the heart of the SI model are two necessary components: SI is tied to course content, and the SI sessions are interactive in nature. Supplemental Instruction sessions give students an opportunity to work collaboratively with the topics presented in a lecture. Because SI leaders are model students who attend each class, they know what has been emphasized during class sessions, how concepts have been presented, and what has not been included. They know how to use the textbook as a resource to go beyond simply following the sample problems. They work the problems for the course and, therefore, know where difficulties lie. SI leaders do not offer study suggestions in isolation, but plan activities that require that all participants struggle with the course material and clarify their understanding of it. SI leaders are not automatic in their responses, but instead build on peer relationships with the students who attend SI sessions, guiding them and challenging their thinking. Successful SI sessions in mathematics, like successful SI sessions in all disciplines, require careful selection and appropriate training and supervision of SI leaders.

As SI supervisors, we have observed many successful SI sessions for mathematics courses. Our analysis of what happened during these effective SI sessions led to our desire to present glimpses of SI sessions. We saw that participants in these sessions felt free to take risks and to try their skills in dealing with mathematics. The SI leaders had planned active learning strategies intended to engage participants with the course material in ways that helped them fill in the gaps in their skills and in their understanding of how to approach problems. This also helped participants realize that there are multiple approaches to solving problems. Look with us at the kinds of things that happened in specific SI sessions in order to see how the collaborative learning in mathematics takes place.

Observations from Supplemental Instruction Sessions

Observation 1. In this glimpse of an SI session, the SI leader focuses on a small part of a lecture. Understanding the definition of the derivative is one of the first new ideas introduced in calculus. What the instructor may have taken five minutes to tell the students about in lecture, the SI leader will encourage the students to talk about until they feel confident in their understanding.

The SI leader has given the students a problem where they need to take the limit of the difference quotient. It seems like magic to them; by doing the algebra, the students think they understand the concept. The SI leader's goal is to make a connection with the slope of the secant line, since without this connection, students will never work the limits with any understanding. The students' work on the board does not include a graph because the students do not think it is important.

The SI leader draws a curve on the board.

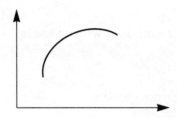

She labels the function, $f(x)$.

SI LEADER: OK, name two points on the curve.
STUDENT A: $(a, f(a))$ and $(b, f(b))$.

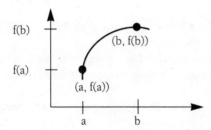

SI LEADER: If we name the first point $(x, f(x))$ instead, what could we name the second point?
STUDENT B: The point is just a little farther on.
SI LEADER: Then can you see that $(x, f(x))$ and $((x + \Delta x), f(x + \Delta x))$ could be equally good names for the points?
STUDENTS: Yes.
SI LEADER: How can you find the slope of the line between the points?
STUDENT C: You would take $f(x + \Delta x) - f(x)$ and divide by Δx.

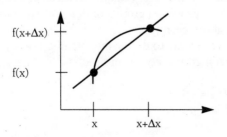

SI LEADER: OK. Does the line that Judy put up there look like you thought the slope of the curve at $(x, f(x))$ would look? What could we do to make the fit better?

STUDENT A: What would happen if we move one of the points, change the value of Δx?

OTHER STUDENT: It gets better as Δx gets smaller.

SI LEADER: How small?

STUDENT C: Let it approach zero.

SI LEADER: Great! What other terms have we used to describe the slope of the curve at a point?

STUDENT D: Slope of the tangent line.

SI LEADER: OK. Good. What else?

STUDENT A: Limit of the difference quotient.

STUDENT B: How about the derivative?

SI LEADER: So, how might we see these in notation?

STUDENT D: $\dfrac{dy}{dx},\ f'(x),\ \lim\limits_{\Delta x \to 0}\ \dfrac{f(x + \Delta x) - f(x)}{\Delta x}$

SI LEADER: That's good. That's how we see it in the book. How do you have it in your notes?

STUDENT E: Dr. Smith wrote $f(x + h)$ using h instead of Δx.

STUDENT B: Oh, is that where that came from!

SI LEADER: Let's divide into three groups. Each group take a piece of the function that we were just looking at. Choose two points and look at the limit.

Finally, one group writes its work on the board and the mechanical grinding out has been put in context.

The SI leader uses probing questions to help the students explore their understanding of the derivative. Students hear their own voices and test their ideas in a safe environment. Exploration, rather than telling, is the focus of the SI. Practical problems like differences in notation between the textbook and the lecture are addressed because the SI leader is in the class and notices that these differences might be confusing to students seeing this notation for the first time. Throughout the session, the SI leader encourages students to talk to each other without waiting for the SI leader to direct the conversation.

Observation 2. This SI session focuses on conic sections. Students were able to understand each type separately, but the SI leader thinks they may have trouble identifying the types within groups of different equations and knowing what is important about each type.

The SI leader asks students to divide into small groups. He passes out a page of equations to each group. For example:

1. $9x^2 + 18x + 4y^2 - 24y = -9$
2. $9x^2 + 18x - 4y^2 + 24y = 63$
3. $(x - 2)^2 = y - 3$

The SI leader asks each group to identify whether each equation represents a straight line, a parabola, a circle, an ellipse, or a hyperbola. The SI leader gives the groups several minutes to discuss their equations. The groups then work together to organize the information they have generated about their equations into a chart summarizing each of the types of equations by identifying the equations, standard forms, important information from the equations, and what the graph looks like.

In the SI session, students develop a matrix that allows them to see patterns emerging. The matrix also allows the students to see connections between ideas. Furthermore, creating a matrix and looking at the interrelationships among these formulas is not something that students are likely to do on their own. As students work together, they share their knowledge and practice using the vocabulary of the discipline to communicate their own discoveries.

Observation 3. Students are trying to understand continuity, differentiability, and the relationship between the two. The SI leader knows that this is the kind of concept that students feel they can grasp one minute but find confusing the next.

The SI leader divides the class into groups of two or three. He gives each group a note card on which he has written statements that the group must refute with an example, explaining graphically if possible. Examples put on note cards:

1. If a function is continuous at X_0, then it is differentiable at X_0.
2. If $f(a) = L$, then $\lim_{x \to a} f(x) = L$.
3. The function $f(x) = [\cos x]$ is continuous everywhere. (Note: [ ] is the greatest integer function. Example: $[1.3] = 1$)

The first group chooses the function $|x - 1|$. Its spokesperson explains that this is not differentiable at $x = 1$; therefore, the statement is false. The graph is continuous (which the spokesperson illustrates by drawing the graph, pointing out that she can draw the graph without lifting her chalk) but is not differentiable.

After the other groups have taken their turns, the discussion continues on the specific rules, to other exceptions to the rules, to how to prove statements that are true.

Using the language of the discipline, students deepen their understanding of concepts and think mathematically. Students express and hear what they and others are thinking about continuity and differentiability. Students spend time grappling with these ideas instead of simply hearing the SI leader give them "the answer." Graphic representations make the ideas stick as students begin to see the connection between the picture and the concept.

Observation 4. Particularly as the semester progresses, the SI leader encourages the students who come to SI to take charge of the session. The SI leader steps back and takes the role of challenging students' thinking. The SI leader encourages students to attempt problems, take the next step, whether that next step is right or wrong. The peer relationship between the students and the SI leader makes it comfortable for students to take risks. Even though doing well in a mathematics course is serious business, SI leaders keep the sessions informal and collegial. During SI sessions, participants have a sense of working hard together with a sense of humor at times; this atmosphere breaks through barriers to risk-taking and to learning.

The SI leader introduces a game: "The name of the game is 'Pass the Chalk.' We'll start with someone reading a problem. The first person to get the chalk will write the problem on the board, and then she will pass the chalk to someone else. When you get the chalk you need to write the next step or, if you think the last step up on the board is wrong, you can correct the last step. Coaching from the audience is encouraged."

As the students work at the board, the students in their seats ask and answer questions about the correct method, allowable shortcuts, and different ways of doing the same step. The SI leader asks students why they did what they did or if they can think of another way to do a step.

One of the SI leader's roles is to be sure that students share more than the mechanics of getting the right answer. Doing the right next step is only half of the task; knowing why you do the next step is just as important. Another function of the SI leader is to be sure that the group is responsible for solving the problem—that is, that no single student becomes stranded at the board, unable to do the next step and feeling threatened.

As students work together, they discover that there is more than one way to do some problems. The focus is on using alternate methods to understand concepts and gaining confidence in seeing why you proceed in a particular way.

Observation 5. An important component of Supplemental Instruction is that students test their own knowledge: "Do I know it or don't I?" SI sessions should include frequent opportunities for students to evaluate their own understanding. This self-testing takes place in many ways as illustrated in our earlier observations. One specific strategy that SI leaders use is the Informal Quiz (Martin, Lorton, Blanc, and Evans, 1977).

The SI leader passes out the Informal Quiz. While working through one particular problem, several students make the same error—not remembering a trigonometric identity. As another student answers this question, the source of their difficulty becomes clear.

The SI leader reinforces the importance of being able to quickly recall the trigonometric identities. Students identify specific knowledge that they need to have at their fingertips to do well in the course. They see that other students in the same class may have a better command of these facts. One of the crucial ideas that an SI leader communicates to students coming to SI is the amount of quality study time required to do well in a mathematics course. This information is invaluable to freshman students because it comes from a peer, the SI leader. Students often do not appreciate the amount of time needed and the importance of daily work for success in a mathematics course.

Observation 6. Students frequently say, "I could do all of the homework problems, but when it came to the test, it was all different!" Supplemental Instruction speaks to this concern by helping students to think ahead of time about what might appear on the exam.

The SI leader has asked students to think about how topics might look on the exam, to predict exam questions. How will this concept appear? Why would the question look like this? Which concepts will a professor link together in a single problem? What wrong turns are we likely to take?

Students are empowered by this activity. The exam isn't a mystery. The more students understand, the more predictable the exam will be for them.

Summary of Observations

In all of the observations we present above, SI leaders guided students in ways that tested their knowledge and led them to greater understanding of mathematical concepts. The activities illustrated in these SI sessions can be generally labeled active learning strategies. The SI leaders did not accidentally happen to use these strategies. Instead, active learning strategies are an integral part of SI training and supervision (Blanc, DeBuhr, and Martin, 1983). SI leaders first experience these strategies during the SI training workshop held prior to the beginning of the term. This workshop is an interactive workshop including actual lectures. Simulated SI sessions run during the SI training workshop offer SI leaders their first opportunity to use active learning strategies creatively. During the training workshop, labels are put on types of strategies; such labels include (as shown in the observations above): using probing questions, sorting concepts into a matrix, explaining or refuting statements on note cards, passing the chalk, the informal quiz, and predicting exam questions. In a way, these strategies are devices to call for full participation from the members of the group; in another way, they are new methods of forcing the kind of categorizing and testing of knowledge that are always a part of "studying."

Lists of such active learning strategies are discussed during the SI training but are only understood when SI leaders see and experience the positive learning that takes place by using the strategies for group study. When mathematics SI leaders complete the SI training workshop, they leave with a basic understanding of how active learning applies to mathematics and with a list of a few particular strategies to use in their SI sessions. The flat lists of active learning strategies discussed during the training workshop come fully to life only as the SI leaders creatively use them to lead their SI groups.

For several weeks following the SI training workshop, the SI supervisor assists the SI leader in planning the sessions. The leader then goes to SI sessions with a plan for what will happen during each session, a plan including possible active learning strategies. The strategies give the SI leader a way to ask for group participation, and in the beginning of the term, the strategies help the SI leader feel secure in taking on the role of leader. This leadership role, however, is always a peer leadership role. Individual participants initially come to SI sessions with an agenda that puts solving the problem and "getting the right answer" far above group participation and moving to a higher level of understanding of mathematics.

If the SI leader solves the problems for the participants, the participants might leave happy with the results, and the SI leader would feel important, but the participants may not have learned how to solve the problem or anything else of importance regarding mathematical concepts. The SI leader could take the role of an expert; she knows how to mirror an instructor's way of demonstrating and explaining solutions to problems, but that teaching method is exactly what the SI leader needs to avoid. She needs instead to maintain the role of a peer leader and to find ways for the participants in the SI sessions to test their approaches to problems, to clarify their thinking, and to explain their thinking to each other. Active learning strategies help SI leaders fulfill their roles as peer leaders, and yet the SI leader must also be flexible enough to scrap all plans if the group needs to move in a different direction. The SI supervisor helps the SI leader experience and see the positive effects of active learning in groups and to allow the group to assume more and more control of the group study activities.

SI leaders possess strong individual talents, yet they need the support of the SI supervisor throughout the term, more extensively at the beginning and continually, to a lesser degree, to the end of the term. All of this comes together nicely as SI leaders approach SI sessions with a creative sense of working with the SI participants to master the course material. The style and creativity of the SI leaders makes SI sessions considerably different from leader to leader. It is the creativity and diversity of SI leaders, along with their capable interpersonal skills, that really make SI work.

References

Blanc, R. A., DeBuhr, L., and Martin, D. C. "Breaking the Attrition Cycle: The Effects of Supplemental Instruction on Undergraduate Performance and Attrition." *Journal of Higher Education*, 1983, 54 (1), 80–89.

Martin, D. C., Arendale, D. (eds.). *Supplemental Instruction: Improving First-Year Student Success in High-Risk Courses*. Columbia, S.C.: National Resource Center for The Freshman Year Experience, 1992.

Martin, D. C., Lorton, M., Blanc, R. A., and Evans, C. *The Learning Center: A Comprehensive Model for Colleges and Universities*. Kansas City, Mo.: University of Missouri, 1977. (ED 162 294)

SANDRA L. BURMEISTER develops study sessions for composition students at Hobart and William Smith Colleges in Geneva, New York, and is a national Supplemental Instruction certified trainer for the University of Missouri–Kansas City.

JEANNE M. CARTER is coordinator in the Academic Skills Center and supervisor of the Supplemental Instruction Program in mathematics and accounting at Oakland University in Rochester, Michigan.

LYNN R. HOCKENBERGER is director of the Academic Skills Center at Oakland University in Rochester, Michigan, and president of the Michigan Tutoring Association.

PATRICIA ANN KENNEY is research associate at the University of Pittsburgh's Learning Research and Development Center.

ANN MCLAREN is coordinator of the Tutoring and the Supplemental Instruction Program at the Pennsylvania State University and a national Supplemental Instruction certified trainer for the University of Missouri–Kansas City.

DORIS L. NICE is director of Learning Assistance and Supplemental Instruction supervisor at the University of Wisconsin-Parkside in Kenosha and a member of the University of Wisconsin Mathematics Placement Committee.

Collaboration, mentoring, and an emphasis on problem solving are key components of a successful Supplemental Instruction program in college chemistry courses.

Supplemental Instruction for College Chemistry Courses

Nancy M. Lockie, Robert J. Van Lanen

In *Achieving Educational Excellence* (1985, p. 3), Alexander Astin argues that improving college teaching relates to one central issue: student involvement. Astin's research findings indicate that "learning will be greatest when the learning environment is structured to encourage active participation by the student." In an effort to involve students more actively in the learning process and to encourage students to assume greater responsibility for their own learning, Supplemental Instruction (SI) has been implemented in these high-risk freshman and sophomore level chemistry courses at Saint Xavier University:

- Chemistry 107—Principles of Inorganic Chemistry and Chemistry 108—Principles of Organic Chemistry and Biochemistry. The university requires this two-semester course sequence of all nursing majors.
- Chemistry 111—General Chemistry I. Chemistry 111 is the first semester of a two-semester course sequence required of all science majors (biology, chemistry, and natural science).
- Chemistry 251–252—Organic Chemistry I and II. This two-semester course sequence meets the needs of science majors.

Our belief is that, if there is to be any chance of improving student success levels in chemistry courses, course faculty and learning assistance personnel must examine and implement collaborative teaching strategies that will enhance the teacher-student relationship and actively involve the student in the learning process. SI strengthens the faculty/student relationship in the following interactive ways:

Course faculty encourage students to attend SI sessions.

Students become actively involved in the course content at SI study sessions.

The SI leader, course faculty, and the SI supervisor meet weekly to focus on how well students understand the material presented in class.

The SI program is evaluated in terms of its impact on student satisfaction/performance as well as on reducing the attrition rate in chemistry courses.

Based on a compilation of over twenty years of research that focused on how college affects students, Pascarella and Terenzini (1991) reported that academic achievement is highest for students who experience favorable faculty relations. Programs such as SI, which involve faculty and students, encourage the formation of such relationships. The research literature documents the effect of collaborative learning in the improvement of both performance and self-esteem of students who are actively involved in the learning process. SI, if collaboratively implemented, has tremendous potential to enhance student learning and problem-solving capabilities in college chemistry courses.

Review of Literature: Skills Needed for Success in College Chemistry Courses

In a recent article, VerBeek and Louters (1991, p. 389) state: "Chemistry is a complex discipline that requires multiple skills to master." They note that chemistry students must be competent in areas such as mathematics, problem solving, conceptualization, theories, and chemical language.

Problem-Solving Strategies. The emphasis in most chemistry courses is on problem solving. Educators have proposed a variety of techniques for enhancing chemistry students' problem-solving skills. Zoller (1987, p. 512) suggests that "the development and encouragement of students' question-asking capability" can significantly contribute to the problem-solving ability of chemistry students. Bodner (1987) and Schrader (1987) discussed the role of algorithms in the problem-solving process. Middlecamp and Kean (1987) suggest dividing chemistry problems into two general categories: generic problems that are solved using a standard procedure, and harder problems that cannot be solved by a simple algorithm. They recommend that the learning strategies needed for problem solving be explicitly taught in college chemistry courses. Many researchers argue that to help students significantly increase their problem-solving skills, it is not sufficient to solely supply them with the conceptual knowledge needed to arrive at a solution but to actively involve students in problem-solving strategies and reasoning that will lead them to the solution (Bransford and Stein, 1984; Genyea, 1983).

Content Mastery in Chemistry. Investigators (Rowe, 1983; Barrow, 1991) believe that students must have command of a specific body of chemical language to solve chemical problems. The ability to master the content of chemistry is another skill required for success in chemistry. Middlecamp and Kean (1988) have described three types of chemical content:

1. Facts, such as, the chemical formula for sulfuric acid is H_2SO_4
2. Concepts, such as pH
3. Rules, such as, bases react with acids to form salts.

Different learning strategies and skills are required to master each type of chemical content: the skills of memorization for learning facts, of classification for mastering concepts, and of application for using rules.

Chemical Language. VerBeek and Louters (1991) found that the difficulties experienced by beginning college chemistry students are largely caused by a lack of chemical language skills rather than a lack of reasoning or mathematical skills. Consistent with these findings, Markow (1988) advocates first teaching students how to speak the language of chemistry, followed by the mathematics and other skills needed to successfully master chemistry.

Supplemental Instruction in Chemistry. Supplemental Instruction that focuses on collaborative learning process, as well as content mastery and active involvement in the learning process, is an ideal learning assistance strategy to enable students with diverse academic and sociocultural backgrounds to master successfully the complex subject of chemistry (Blanc, DeBuhr, and Martin, 1983; Martin and Arendale, 1992). However, there is little research in the literature that focuses on the implementation and impact of SI specifically in chemistry courses. Lundeberg (1990) has reported a study measuring the effect of SI on student performance in a college level chemistry course and describing the students' reactions to the program and to the learning environment of the SI sessions. Her findings, as measured by final grades in chemistry and responses to a questionnaire, demonstrated that SI was effective in increasing students' achievement in chemistry. In a study of the impact of Supplemental Instruction on student performance in Chemistry 108 (Principles of Organic and Biochemistry) at Saint Xavier University, significant differences in student performance in the course, as measured by final grades, were observed for the SI group versus the non-SI group. The SI group consisted of students attending six or more SI sessions during the semester, and the non-SI group consisted of students attending five or fewer SI sessions (Van Lanen and Lockie, 1992; Lockie and Van Lanen, 1993).

Customization of the Supplemental Instruction Model for Chemistry Courses

In adapting the SI model for use in chemistry courses, we have identified the following components: selection of effective SI leaders and SI supervisors; collaboration among SI team members; and development of appropriate strategies for SI study sessions.

Characteristics of the Ideal SI Supervisor. In many programs, SI supervisors are members of the academic support services on campus. In our case, whenever possible, SI supervisors are faculty members whose discipline is the same as the majority of the students in the course (for example, in Chemistry

107 and 108, SI supervisors are nursing faculty members; in Chemistry 111, the SI supervisor is a science faculty member). These faculty members are, in our opinion, the most effective SI supervisors because they provide an important and unique mentoring role for students in the specific chemistry courses supported by SI. The SI supervisor and SI leader meet with students on the first day of class to introduce the SI model and indicate their availability as resources for the students. The course instructor is also available outside of class, as usual, to all students who may seek assistance. Secondly, on the first day of class, SI supervisors share with students their experiences as students in chemistry courses. For example, their realization that the study of chemistry was challenging and required a great deal more study time than they first anticipated; their feelings of being "overwhelmed" on the first day of class; how they approached the study of chemistry; and time management strategies that worked for them. SI supervisors also discuss the importance of chemistry in their discipline and provide concrete examples of how chemistry is applied in their discipline. The mentoring by the SI supervisor enhances student motivation to study and learn chemistry. The use of nursing and science faculty as SI supervisors also gives students an opportunity to get to know a faculty member in their major on an informal basis. The research by Pascarella and Terenzini (1991) on student interaction with faculty notes that this interaction is a potentially important influence on learning. The work of Endo and Harpel (1982) confirmed the notion that the frequency of informal contact with faculty also had a statistically positive association with freshmen's report of their knowledge of basic facts.

The Collaborative Process and the SI Supervisor. The SI supervisor assumes the role of facilitator to enable the collaborative process to occur. The collaborative process involving the course instructor, SI supervisor, and the SI leader is ongoing and consistent throughout the entire semester, beginning with the initial training sessions in which all members of this team are present and in the periodic meetings held regularly throughout the semester. The course instructors add to the richness of the training sessions in several ways. Their presence assures SI leaders of the course instructor's commitment to SI and provides the informal contact and collegiality between the course instructor and SI leader that may not occur in a typical student-teacher relationship. Some of the SI leader's comments validate the course instructor's teaching style. For example, at one training session an SI leader spoke about students' needs in the area of mathematics competency and problem-solving skills which evoked affirmative nods from the course instructor in that particular chemistry course. The SI leader indicated to the instructor that this would be the focus of the SI study sessions during the first two weeks of Chemistry 107. At the weekly meetings during the semester, student progress in the course, student concerns about the course, the progress of the SI sessions, and strategies for future SI sessions are discussed; but the names of students who participated in the SI sessions are not given to the course instructor. From the SI supervisor's perspective, the course instructor who is involved in the process supports SI in a more aggressive manner than the course instructor who simply wants

SI to be offered in his or her course but does not want to be involved in the dynamics of a collaborative process.

The SI supervisor meets several times with the class during the course of the semester (for example, after hour exams) to get student feedback on the course and the SI sessions and to share with students the performance of the SI group versus the non-SI group on hour exams. The SI supervisor invites students who are doing poorly in the course to meet with him or her to discuss the problems they are having with the course.

Another example of the collaborative process involves the use of SI student advocates who have successfully completed the chemistry course. At the beginning of the semester, the SI supervisor introduces these supportive students. They speak to the class about their experiences in SI and how SI helped them to succeed in the course. These ten-minute presentations enhance student motivation for attending SI sessions.

Characteristics of the Ideal SI Leader. In our application of Supplemental Instruction in chemistry courses, we find that the most effective SI leaders are students whose academic major is the same as the majority of the students in the class (for example, SI leaders for Chemistry 107 and 108 are nursing majors and SI leaders for Chemistry 111 and Chemistry 251 are science majors). This connection provides an important mentoring role for the SI leader. In Chemistry 107 and Chemistry 108, many students are able to relate to the SI leader as a peer and mentor, since they are all nursing majors. Such an SI leader tends to be more understanding of and sympathetic to the struggle required for students to succeed in the course and is able to document the applicability of chemistry to the students' major. Comments from SI leaders, as reported in SI leader surveys conducted at the end of the course, support the importance of the SI leader's mentoring role as a motivational factor.

The Collaborative Process and the SI Leader. Regular interaction with the SI supervisor and the course instructor allows the SI leader to provide feedback on how the SI study sessions are progressing and what course content the students appear to be having problems with. The course instructor can use this feedback to make suggestions on strategies to be used in future SI sessions and to further illustrate a particular topic in the next class. For students who understood the concept the first time, the instructor's use of feedback provides reinforcement. To other students, it clarifies and expands previously presented course content. The SI supervisor and the SI leader visit the classroom after each exam to provide support and encouragement to the students. They stress the need for regular and consistent attendance at SI study sessions and urge the students to examine their individual study habits and make modifications as needed.

Strategies and Materials Used in Study Sessions

The SI leader's aim in the SI study sessions is to assist students in identifying a cognitive map of strategies that will lead them toward success in studying chemistry. Some of the strategies used with success in various chemistry SI sessions follow.

Problem Solving. The hallmark of chemistry SI sessions is their emphasis on the use of a problem-solving approach to learning and applying chemistry content. On the average, 70 to 80 percent of the time in SI sessions is devoted to problem solving. The problems used in SI sessions come from problem sets provided by the instructor, assigned problems in the text, and, in some cases, problems prepared by the SI leaders. For example, in Chemistry 108, problem sets focus on the structure, nomenclature, properties, reactions, and synthesis of the various classes of organic compounds. In biochemistry, problems focus on the structure and properties of biomolecules, bioenergetics, and the primary metabolic pathways.

SI students are encouraged to organize their approach to solving problems by following a logical series of steps:

1. Identify what the problem is asking.
2. Decide what information is needed to solve the problem.
3. Correctly apply the information to solve the problem.
4. Go over the answer to the problem to verify that it is reasonable.

For example, in naming organic compounds, students work at the blackboard. They learn to make sure they have drawn the structure given in the problem correctly, to identify what the organic functional group or groups are, to pick out the parent chain and name it, and then to name and specify the positions of any substituents. One successful method SI students use in solving problems is to recall how previous problems were solved and to keep building on previously learned methods and information.

SI leaders structure problem solving in SI sessions in several different ways, depending on the needs of the students. In some cases the entire group works on solving a problem with one student member at the blackboard to write down the solution. In other cases, individual students are assigned a problem or problems to work individually at the blackboard simultaneously. After a period of time, the individual students are asked to explain their solution(s) to the problem(s) they worked on to the entire group, which then makes corrections and verifies that each proposed solution is correct. If a particular student is unable to solve the assigned problem or problems, then the entire group works on the problem(s). In another approach to the above activity, teams of students, rather than individuals, are assigned or volunteer to do particular problems at the blackboard. In another approach, students are asked to list problems they are having difficulty with on the blackboard at the beginning of the SI session. The SI group then works on these problems. In rare cases, when the entire group is "stuck" on a given problem, the SI leader may offer suggestions on how to proceed. If this approach does not produce positive results, the SI leader may solve the problem, explain the answer, and then give the students several similar problems to work on. Occasionally, problem-solving competitions are held during SI sessions. Students are divided into teams and each team is assigned a set of problems to solve. The team that solves the most problems correctly and can explain their solutions to the entire group wins the competition.

There are several advantages to using problem solving in chemistry SI sessions. First it actively engages students in the study of chemistry. Second, it increases students' awareness that, in order to solve problems, one needs to know the basic factual content of the chemistry course. Third, it helps students learn basic chemistry content and reinforces their understanding of content, especially when students have to explain "their solution" to the other SI members. Fourth, successful problem solving builds students' confidence in their ability to master and use the content of chemistry. Fifth, problem solving enhances the critical thinking abilities of students. Student evaluations of the SI program strongly support the value of the problem-solving approach in SI sessions. When students were asked on final evaluations of the SI program to identify the most valuable learning strategy used in the chemistry SI sessions, they most frequently responded that it was working problems on the blackboard (refer to section on Students' Evaluation of the SI Program later in this chapter). In SI Leader evaluations of the SI program, SI leaders also identified that doing problems at the blackboard was the most helpful strategy for students in the SI study sessions.

Learning the Factual Content of Chemistry. Successful chemistry students need to be able to recall the factual content of chemistry quickly and accurately. SI leaders share with students some of the strategies they used to master chemistry factual content. One strategy is the use of note cards summarizing basic chemical facts, for example, chemical formulas and names for ions, names and symbols for the elements, the reactions of alkenes, the structures of monosaccharides, and so on. As an example, one SI leader has students make up one note card for each organic functional group. The note cards contain the general formula, characteristic properties, and reactions of the functional group as well as tests observed for the functional group in the laboratory. Students can use note cards for study in traveling to and from school, at work, and at other times for memorization and recall techniques. Another key to the mastery of chemical facts is the organization of the facts into a whole. In Chemistry 108, one SI study group spent several sessions preparing a "map" of the major metabolic pathways covered in lecture. This map allowed students to appreciate the relationships among the individual metabolic pathways, for example, how glycolysis relates to the tricarboxylic acid cycle and electron transport/oxidative phosphorylation; how the catabolism of triglycerides relates to the glycolytic pathway; the relationship of amino acid catabolism to the tricarboxylic acid cycle. Students who participated in this exercise claim it was a major factor in their finally understanding and appreciating what metabolism is all about. Another strategy used by some SI leaders is to have the students in SI sessions prepare a review sheet for each exam. In some cases, the SI leader prepares the review sheet listing main concepts, and students in SI sessions explain and discuss each of the concepts on the review sheet.

Breaking Down the Chemical Language Barrier. The terminology and language associated with the study of chemistry represents a significant obstacle to student success in chemistry courses. One strategy successfully used by SI study groups to break down the chemical language barrier is the development by students in SI sessions of a chemical language dictionary. In the first week of class, students begin writing in their notebook the chemical term and its meaning the first time the professor uses it. The students arrange their dictionary in alphabetical order to enable easy access. Another strategy that is designed to enhance the students' learning is to have students explain the meaning of chemical terms to each other in their own words.

Quizzes. Several SI leaders have developed and utilized five-minute quizzes on the lecture material and the problem sets for the week. At the beginning of the SI session, the students individually take the quiz. The SI leader then divides them into groups with each group being responsible for one quiz question. Each group is responsible for working out the "answer" to the particular quiz question, presenting and explaining the answer to the entire group, and having the entire group come to a consensus on the correct answer to the particular quiz question. Practice quizzes are very popular with chemistry SI students, and they do have the advantage of reducing test anxiety.

Hints for Success. In the first SI session, SI leaders make practical suggestions on some of the types of behavior that in their experience are associated with success in the particular chemistry course. For example, an SI leader in Chemistry 111 distributed the following handout in the first SI session:

Some Suggestions for Enhancing Performance in Chemistry 111
1. Attend all lectures.
2. Read assignments before coming to class.
3. Bring the textbook to class every day.
4. Pay specific attention to handouts and transparencies.
5. Know how to use a calculator.
6. Review basic algebra skills.
7. Know how to construct and interpret graphs.
8. Show all math steps (regardless of how trivial) when solving problems and writing up lab reports.
9. Attend SI sessions on a consistent basis.

While many of these suggestions may seem obvious to the reader, they are not necessarily obvious to all students taking Chemistry 111 or other chemistry courses.

Basic Skills Enhancement. In the first several SI sessions of the semester, SI leaders help students identify their individual learning needs in the areas of mathematics competency, operation of a calculator, time-management skills, note-taking skills, text-reading skills, and test anxiety. Following are some strategies used with success in various chemistry SI sessions to enhance some of the basic skills needed to succeed in chemistry:

- *Mathematics competency and calculator skills.* The SI leaders for Chemistry 107 and Chemistry 111 schedule extra SI study sessions for those students who need help in mathematics competency and calculator skills. Students are encouraged to use computer software packages in basic algebra and basic mathematical computations that are available in the Learning Assistance Center. The SI leader emphasizes that the student must be competent in these areas within the first two weeks of class in order to be successful in chemistry.

- *Time-management skills.* The SI leader shares with the students how he or she managed "time" and the amount of study time required in order to study chemistry successfully. A semester calendar is used to organize course tests and assignments; work schedules; commuting time to the university; and realistic home, sleep, and recreation requirements. Each student utilizes this calendar to plan a time-management schedule for the semester. Time management is a significant component of success in chemistry courses. SI leaders, in end-of-semester surveys, reported the development of time-management skills as one of the important behaviors they learned from participation in the SI program.

- *Note-taking skills.* Many students frequently speak of feeling "overwhelmed" and "confused" in the SI sessions after leaving chemistry lectures. The lecture notes, handouts, and overhead transparencies are used as content organizers to assist students in the development of note-taking skills. The integration of the chapters in the text to the lecture notes, handouts, and transparencies is essential to grasp early in the course.

- *Text-reading skills.* Students learn to break down the whole (lecture notes, overheads, and text-reading for a particular lecture) into manageable "chunks" of material. Some of the strategies employed by SI groups include the following:

Link the diagrams and illustrations in the text with the text writing and to lecture notes.

Recognize that new terms are usually italicized and in bold print when they first occur in a chapter.

At a minimum, skim chapters for general content before lectures.

- *Test-taking anxiety.* The students talk about how they feel taking tests and how they study for tests. The use of the Learning Assistance Center as a resource for test-taking strategies and for strategies to reduce test-taking anxiety are emphasized. The SI leader shares that many students attest to difficulty in taking tests and that this is a concern for all students. The notion of the SI study session as a support group is continually referred to throughout the semester. Talking things over with classmates and studying together for tests can build confidence and reduce test anxiety.

Research on Students' Evaluation of Supplemental Instruction

The main purpose of this study is to help SI supervisors and SI leaders learn how SI is perceived by SI participants. The sample ($N = 219$) consisted of all students enrolled in SI-supported chemistry courses from Spring 1990 through Fall 1992. All students in the SI-supported chemistry courses were invited to participate in the SI program. One hundred and thirty students (59 percent) participated in one or more SI study sessions during the semester in which they were enrolled in an SI-supported chemistry course. Participants in the SI program were asked to complete an end-of-semester written evaluation tool on the last day of class. Some of the questions that were asked are listed and student responses are reported as group data and as "direct quotes."

1. *What aspects of SI were particularly helpful to you in enhancing your performance in chemistry?* Student responses to this question were organized into three general themes: strategies, the SI leader's role, and the SI study sessions.

Strategies. Many students reported that using the blackboard for problems was one of the best parts of SI. One student stated that working out problems on the board until she understood it was helpful to her. Another student reported that "the SI leader did not just tell you the answer. You had to work to get it." The majority of students cited that using "group discussions" helped them to prepare for tests. Other students felt that talking through difficult concepts in language they could understand, getting different points of view, and learning different study strategies were very helpful to them.

SI Leader Role. Many students reported that the SI leader listened to their opinions and altered the format of the SI study session accordingly. Other students stated that the material was easier to understand because it was discussed at a slower pace than in course lectures that allow them to understand difficult concepts.

SI Study Sessions. Students stated that learning "shortcuts" and other study strategies from other students, working with students who knew more and some who knew less, and focusing on what was important were benefits of the SI sessions. Based on the evaluation comments, students felt comfortable in the SI study sessions and indicated that the small groups made it easier to ask questions. The majority of students indicated that the SI study sessions were valuable to them.

2. *How can the SI program be improved?* Approximately one-third of the respondents felt that there should be more time slots available for SI and more SI leaders to conduct additional sessions. Many students felt that no improvement was needed: "It just needs to be promoted more. It is extremely helpful and needs to be emphasized." Some students suggested a more structured format and were uncomfortable when they were asked to prepare for study sessions. Others felt that advanced students should be separated from the slow students; each have different needs.

3. *Should the Supplemental Instruction program be continued?* The target population ($N = 219$) consisted of all students enrolled in SI-supported chemistry courses from Spring 1990 through Fall 1992. Of this number 98 percent urged that the SI program be continued for chemistry students.

Conclusions

Based on our experience, SI is an effective strategy for enhancing student performance in lower division chemistry courses. However, consistent and frequent student participation in SI sessions is essential for SI to have a measurable impact on student performance. Active collaboration among the course instructor, SI leader, SI supervisor, and students is vital to the success of the SI experience in chemistry. Student and SI leader evaluation data indicate the merit of active student involvement in the learning process and the effectiveness of problem solving as an important learning strategy for mastering chemistry content. Students are enthusiastic about the SI program and overwhelmingly recommend that it be continued. We are currently exploring ways to improve the frequency and consistency of student attendance at SI sessions.

References

Astin, A. W. *Achieving Educational Excellence: A Critical Assessment of Priorities and Practices in Higher Education.* San Francisco: Jossey-Bass, 1985.

Barrow, G. M. "Learning Chemistry." *Journal of Chemical Education,* 1991, *68* (6), 449–453.

Blanc, R. A., DeBuhr, L. E., and Martin, D. C. "Breaking the Attrition Cycle: The Effects of Supplemental Instruction on Undergraduate Performance and Attrition." *Journal of Higher Education,* 1983, *54* (1), 80–89.

Bodner, G. M. "The Role of Algorithms in Teaching Problem Solving." *Journal of Chemical Education,* 1987, *64* (6), 513–514.

Bransford, J. D., and Stein, B. S. *The IDEAL Problem Solver.* New York: W. H. Freeman, 1984.

Endo, J., and Harpel, R. "The Effect of Student-Faculty Interaction on Students' Educational Outcomes." *Research in Higher Education,* 1982, *16,* 115–138.

Genyea, J. "Improving Students' Problem Solving Skills." *Journal of Chemical Education,* 1983, *60* (5), 478–482.

Lockie, N. M., and Van Lanen, R. J. "Improving the Retention and Performance of Nursing Students in Chemistry: A Peer Collaborative Learning Process." Paper presented at Sigma Theta Tau International, 32nd Biennial Convention, Indianapolis, Indiana, 1993.

Lundeberg, M. A. "Supplemental Instruction in Chemistry." *Journal of Research in Science Teaching,* 1990, *27* (2), 145–155.

Markow, A. "Teaching Chemistry Like the Foreign Language It Is." *Journal of Chemical Education,* 1988, *65* (4), 346–347.

Martin, D. C., Arendale, D. (eds.). *Supplemental Instruction: Improving First-Year Student Success in High-Risk Courses.* Columbia, S.C.: National Resource Center for the Freshman Year Experience, 1992.

Middlecamp, C., and Kean, K. "Problems and 'That Other Stuff': Types of Chemical Content." *Journal of Chemical Education,* 1988, *65* (1), 53–56.

Middlecamp, C., and Kean, K. "Generic and Harder Problems: Teaching Problem Solving." *Journal of Chemical Education*, 1987, *64* (6), 516–517.

Pascarella, E., and Terenzini, P. *How College Affects Students*. San Francisco: Jossey-Bass, 1991.

Rowe, M. "Getting Chemistry Off the Killer Course List." *Journal of Chemical Education*, 1983, *60* (11), 954–956.

Schrader, C. L. "Using Algorithms to Teach Problem Solving." *Journal of Chemical Education*, 1987, *64* (6), 518–520.

Van Lanen, R. J., and Lockie, N. M. "Addressing the Challenge of Student Diversity: The Impact of Supplemental Instruction on Performance in a Freshman Level Chemistry Course." Unpublished paper, Department of Science and School of Nursing, Saint Xavier University, 1992.

Ver Beek, K., and Louters, L. "Chemical Language Skills." *Journal of Chemical Education*, 1991, *68* (5), 389–391.

Zoller, U. "The Fostering of Question-Asking Capability." *Journal of Chemical Education*, 1987, *64* (6), 510–512.

NANCY M. LOCKIE is associate professor of nursing and a Supplemental Instruction supervisor at Saint Xavier University in Chicago.

ROBERT J. VAN LANEN is associate professor of chemistry and a Supplemental Instruction supervisor at Saint Xavier University in Chicago.

Findings from research studies provide some evidence that participation in Supplemental Instruction programs can have an effect in the following areas for students: course grades, rates of D and F grades and course withdrawals, and semester grade-point averages.

Research Studies on the Effectiveness of Supplemental Instruction in Mathematics

Patricia Ann Kenney, James M. Kallison, Jr.

Recent documents from the National Council of Teachers of Mathematics (1989) and the National Research Council (1991) have emphasized the need for mathematical literacy. Yet for many undergraduate students, mathematics has become a filter rather than a pump in that lack of success in mathematics often prevents students from entering scientific and professional careers. In a document that advocates sweeping changes in the way undergraduate mathematics is taught, the members of the Committee on the Mathematical Sciences in the Year 2000 present an action plan that promulgates effective instructional models that foster learning about learning and involving students actively in the learning process (National Research Council, 1991). A Supplemental Instruction (SI) program has the potential to provide academic support for students in entry-level undergraduate mathematics courses that aligns with the goals for change in mathematics instruction. This chapter begins with a brief summary of the theoretical foundations of the SI model and then details results from research studies on the effectiveness of SI programs, with an emphasis on studies in college-level mathematics.

Theoretical Foundations for Supplemental Instruction

Other chapters in this volume provide detailed information on Supplemental Instruction, including a summary of its theoretical foundations. However, studies in the area of mathematics learning have suggested at least one additional theoretical framework for SI.

NEW DIRECTIONS FOR TEACHING AND LEARNING, no. 60, Winter 1994 © Jossey-Bass Publishers

Blanc, DeBuhr, and Martin (1983) believe that the theoretical basis for the Supplemental Instruction model involves a developmental viewpoint based on Piagetian principles. While this link to Piaget is certainly reasonable, Kenney's (1988) analysis of the basic tenets of SI reveals an interesting connection to cognitive psychology, especially to the area of metacognition. According to Flavell, metacognition refers to "one's knowledge of one's own cognitive processes" (1976, p. 232) and to the active monitoring and regulation of these processes. The concept of a control system that oversees the mental flow of information best exemplifies the monitoring aspect. Gagné, an educational psychologist, called this process executive control (1983); Skemp, a mathematics educator and researcher, labeled it reflective intelligence (1980). Others in the field of mathematics (for example, Burton, 1984; Garofalo and Lester, 1985) have suggested that metacognitive strategies could be incorporated into the study of mathematics learning. It is interesting to note that these and other researchers agree on the positive relationship between a well-developed cognitive monitoring system and the effective use of learning strategies. They also advocate that students can be taught such strategies, which are most beneficial when introduced in the context of a particular academic subject. Since the link between learning strategies and course content forms the basis for the Supplemental Instruction model, the connection between SI as practice and metacognition as its theoretical base becomes more plausible.

Studies on the Effectiveness of Supplemental Instruction

Some research studies exist on the effects of student participation in a Supplemental Instruction program. Early reports and monographs (Martin, 1980; Martin, Lorton, Blanc, and Evans, 1977) detailed student achievement levels by using descriptive statistics. Results from another report (Martin and Blanc, 1980) documented the first longitudinal investigation on the effects of an SI program. Martin and Blanc found that those students who participated in SI sessions for an American history course showed patterns of higher course grades and higher rates of retention in college. Results from three case studies (Martin, Blanc, and DeBuhr, 1983) and a journal article (Wolfe, 1987) indicated similar patterns of success.

Most of the studies mentioned thus far used small samples or did not employ inferential statistics in reporting results. Blanc, DeBuhr, and Martin (1983) conducted the first large-scale investigation of the effects of participation in a Supplemental Instruction program. Using a sample of more than 700 students enrolled in at least one of four courses, these researchers found that, when compared to classmates who chose not to attend the extra sessions or who could not attend due to scheduling conflicts, the SI·participants had significantly higher final course grades and semester grade point averages. Moreover, by tracking these students for an additional two semesters, it was found that SI participants had a higher frequency of reenrollment in college. Based on these results, Blanc and his colleagues concluded that Supplemental Instruction is an effective program that can affect a student's achievement level in college courses, rate of retention in college, and, ultimately, the likelihood of earning a baccalaureate degree.

In a more recent series of quasi-experimental studies, Martin, Arendale, and associates used information from students in 190 courses at the University of Missouri–Kansas City (UMKC) offering SI during the time period from 1980 to 1991. The treatment group consisted of students who voluntarily participated in SI; the control group consisted of non-SI participants. Results from this study were that at UMKC, SI participants "earned a significantly higher percentage of A & B final course grades, earned a significantly lower percentage of D & F final course grades and withdrawals, and earned significantly higher mean final course grades than the non-SI participants" (Martin and Arendale, 1992, p. 21). On a more global level, Martin and her colleagues analyzed data from forty-nine institutions and obtained results similar to the findings from the UMKC sample.

It is important to note that investigating the effects of SI in particular academic subject areas was not the purpose of the UMKC studies. A few research studies, however, have investigated the effects of SI in particular college-level courses. For example, Pryor (1989) used 268 students enrolled in three high-risk science courses (animal biology, plant biology, introductory physics). She found that attendance at SI sessions related significantly to final course grades, that students who attended SI earned significantly higher final course grades than students who did not attend SI, and that there was a significant difference in the grade distribution of students who attended SI and who did not attend. In her study of SI in a college chemistry course, Lundeberg (1990) found that SI was effective in increasing students' achievement as measured by final course grades and students' responses to a questionnaire.

It is also important to note that in all of the above studies, a lack of a "true" control group prevented the conclusion that the superior performance of the SI group was due to the unique benefits of participation in an SI program. Perhaps students in the SI group earned higher grades because the group participation systematically exposed them to the course material more rather than because they experienced the benefits of a program that combined appropriate study skills with course content.

Studies on the Effectiveness of Supplemental Instruction in Mathematics

Given the emphasis on the need to succeed in college-level mathematics courses, it is important to study the effects of participation in Supplemental Instruction programs geared toward an entry-level mathematics course such as calculus. In one of her early studies, Kenney (1988) utilized two intact classes of a college-level calculus course for business majors. In order to control for instructor effects, a single mathematics instructor was assigned to both large lecture classes, each divided into three discussion (recitation) sections: students in one set of two "treatment" discussion sections experienced SI; students in the other set of two "control" discussion sections did not. Students in the remaining two discussion sections did not participate in the study. In the treatment sections, Kenney performed the duties of an SI leader; in the control sections, she performed the duties typical to a graduate teaching assistant (that is, content-based discussion only). Kenney created and implemented an observation instrument to control for the threat of experimenter bias inherent in this model. Statistical assurances confirmed group equivalence with respect to a set of important independent variables such as mathematics ability and achievement levels, high school class rank, gender, and college of enrollment. Using a variety of statistical techniques, Kenney found that students who had experienced SI had significantly higher final course grades and semester grade point averages than the students in the non-SI group (1989) and that the SI students had a lower level of D or F grades and course withdrawals (1990). However, SI was not the only contributing factor to student success. High school class rank, discussion section attendance, and test scores from instruments that measured mathematics ability and achievement were also significant variables.

In a follow-up study, Kenney tracked the students in the original studies in order to investigate their course-taking patterns and to check for differences in second-semester business calculus course grades. No SI program was available during the follow-up study semester, and students enrolled in a number of different sections of the second-semester calculus course. The results showed no differences in course-taking patterns between the two groups, and no significant difference between their final course grades in the second-semester course (Kenney, 1990).

To date, the Kenney studies are unique in that they (1) examined SI in mathematics courses, (2) used a graduate student (herself) as an SI leader, and (3) used regularly scheduled discussion sections (vis-à-vis adjunct meeting times established during the first week of class) for both the control and treatment groups. However, the potential threat of experimenter bias limited these studies. Thus, Kallison and Kenney (1992) planned another series of studies using students in entry-level calculus courses and using graduate teaching assistants (TA's) as the SI leaders.

These studies were conducted at the University of Texas at Austin during the Fall 1989 semester. The two TA's were mathematics graduate students selected and trained for the SI program by the staff of the university's Learning Skills Center (LSC). Their ten hours of preservice training focused on three areas: (1) the Supplemental Instruction model itself and general principles for SI implementation, (2) the relevant study skills needed for students in mathematics, and (3) potential methods to integrate SI techniques into discussions of course content. After training sessions were over, an LSC staff member, serving as SI Supervisor, continued to meet with the two TA's once a week during the semester. These supervisory meetings allowed the TA's to share and discuss the SI techniques they were attempting to integrate into their discussion sections, and the TA's received useful feedback from each other and from the SI supervisor about strategies they were using and problems they were experiencing. These meetings also gave the SI supervisor opportunities to reinforce principles brought out in preservice training as well as to plan potential strategies to be used later in the semester.

In the case of the classes involved in these studies, extreme care was taken to confirm that the comparison groups (that is, "SI group" and "non-SI group") of students were equivalent with respect to a set of important quantitative and qualitative variables. The former set of variables included standardized test scores from mathematics ability and achievement measures, while the latter set included factors such as gender, ethnicity, class in school, and college of enrollment.

In order to evaluate the effectiveness of SI, a comparison of mean course grades was made between students in the SI and non-SI groups. The grades were based upon performances on three tests given during the semester and a final exam. Mean course grades were also used as the outcome measure in evaluating the interaction effects of SI with ability and achievement levels in mathematics.

Study 1: Calculus for Business Students. The first study compared the performance of 239 students in two large lecture classes of a business calculus course, both taught during the Fall 1989 semester. The same instructor taught these classes, which met at consecutive time periods (12:00 and 1:00 P.M.). For each lecture class, students were assigned to one of three TA-led discussion sections that met twice a week during the entire semester. The average class size in a discussion section was thirty-five. While the students in the two classes had different TA's for their discussion sections, their tests and final exam were the same. The TA assigned to the noon lecture class received training in SI techniques and utilized the SI model in conducting his three discussion sessions (the SI group); the TA assigned to the 1 P.M. class did not receive training in SI and conducted his three discussion sections (the non-SI group) with a traditional content-only focus. None of the students knew they were participants in a study.

Results from the investigation of the quantitative and qualitative variables showed that the SI group and non-SI group were equivalent with respect to general ability and mathematics achievement levels and that there were no significant gender, ethnicity, class, or college of enrollment differences between the groups. The majority of students in both groups were majoring in business and were either freshmen or sophomores.

Results of a comparison between the groups' final grades in the business calculus course showed that the average course grade for the SI group (2.39) was significantly different from that of the non-SI student group (1.96). While these results could be due to differences in general teaching effectiveness between the two TA's (vis-à-vis the effect of Supplemental Instruction), the results were nevertheless encouraging.

Kallison and Kenney investigated an additional question: With respect to mathematics, do lower-ability students benefit more from SI than do higher-ability students? A statistically significant interaction between scores on a test of quantitative ability (that is, SAT quantitative score) and final course grades emerged. One interpretation of this finding follows: exposure to SI techniques appeared to help the lower-ability students disproportionately more than the higher-ability students.

Study 2: Calculus for Engineering and Natural Science Students. The second study compared the performance of 241 students in two large lecture classes of a calculus course geared toward engineering and the natural sciences (hereafter called "engineering calculus"). While the same instructor taught both classes and the same TA led all of the discussion groups, the classes were from two different semesters. One class met during the Fall 1988 semester. At that time, the TA had no training in SI techniques and, therefore, conducted his three discussion sections (the non-SI group) using a traditional content-only focus. However, in the Fall 1989 semester, this same TA used SI techniques in his three discussions sections (the SI group). Although the two courses were offered in different semesters, the instructor confirmed that his instructional presentations were the same and that his tests were equivalent for the two courses. Further, the two classes and discussion sections met at the identical times of the day. As was the case for Study 1, none of the students knew they were participants in a study.

Results from the investigation of the quantitative and qualitative variables showed that the SI group and non-SI group were equivalent with respect to general ability and mathematics achievement levels and that there were no significant differences between the groups in gender, ethnicity, class, or college of enrollment. The majority of students in both groups were majoring in engineering and were either freshmen or sophomores.

Results from a comparison between the groups on final grades in the engineering calculus course showed that the average course grade for the SI group (2.00) and the non-SI group (1.91) were not significantly different. It is worth noting that an important limitation to the interpretations of these results stems from the fact that the data were collected one year apart.

As in Study 1, Kallison and Kenney investigated the effects of participation (or nonparticipation) in SI for students at different levels of mathematical ability or achievement for engineering calculus students. While a significant interaction again occurred, this time it was between scores on a test of mathematics achievement in algebra and trigonometry topics and final course grades. One interpretation of this result follows: As was found in Study 1, exposure to SI appeared to help the lower-achieving students disproportionately more than the higher-achieving students. It is interesting to note that, instead of the mathematical ability measure, the mathematics achievement measure was the significant independent variable in this interaction study.

Discussion

Many colleges and universities use SI as a means to enhance undergraduate education and to reduce attrition rates in high-risk courses. The research studies on the effects of SI programs in calculus courses add to the empirical base for SI in some important ways. First, it supports previous research (Kenney, 1988, 1989, 1990) on the effectiveness of an SI program in entry-level mathematics courses. While the possibility of "teacher" effect was a significant limitation in Study I, which used two teaching assistants, note that the TA's for both the SI discussion sections and traditional discussion sections did have some common characteristics such as similar mathematical backgrounds and prior teaching experiences.

This research is also significant in that the presence of an interaction between SI and non-SI group membership and measures of mathematics achievement and aptitude is unique to this study and supports the hypothesis that SI provides disproportionate assistance to lower-ability students. This finding may suggest that the higher-ability students are more capable of determining on their own appropriate ways of learning the subject area than are the lower-ability students. Or perhaps, the higher-ability students feel that any information that they perceive as non-content related is not useful. Another rationale for the result is that the higher-ability students are indeed attentive during these times and utilize the information and become much more efficient learners than they would be otherwise. Thus, SI may not significantly improve grades for higher-ability learners, but it could result in less studying time for them.

Results from this study also provide a rationale for including a study skills component (if not an entire SI program) as part of the training for graduate teaching assistants. The use of TA's as SI leaders appears to be a promising direction. Additional research should evaluate the effectiveness of SI in other disciplines. These studies should also incorporate interaction analyses so that educators can determine those populations that are most helped by SI. Supplemental Instruction remains an important model in teaching learning skills through discipline-specific discussion sections.

References

Blanc, R., DeBuhr, L., and Martin, D. C. "Breaking the Attrition Cycle: The Effects of Supplemental Instruction on Undergraduate Performance and Attrition." *Journal of Higher Education,* 1983, *54* (1), 80–90.

Burton, L. "Mathematical Thinking: The Struggle for Meaning." *Journal for Research in Mathematics Education,* 1984, *15* (1), 35–49.

Flavell, J. H. "Metacognitive Aspects of Problem Solving." In L. Resnick (ed.), *The Nature of Intelligence,* Hillsdale, N.J.: Lawrence Erlbaum, 1976.

Gagné, R. M. "Some Issues in the Psychology of Mathematics Instruction." *Journal for Research in Mathematics Education,* 1983, *14* (1), 7–18.

Garofalo, J., and Lester, F. K. "Metacognition, Cognitive Monitoring, and Mathematical Performance." *Journal for Research in Mathematics Education,* 1985, *16* (3), 163–176.

Kallison, J. M., and Kenney, P. A. "Learning to Study College-Level Mathematics: Effects of a Supplemental Instruction (SI) Program in a First-Semester Calculus Course." Paper presented at the American Educational Research Association Conference, San Francisco, Apr. 1992.

Kenney, P. A. "Effects of Supplemental Instruction (SI) on Student Performance in a College-Level Mathematics Course." Unpublished doctoral dissertation, Mathematics Education Division, Department of Curriculum and Instruction, University of Texas at Austin, 1988.

Kenney, P. A. "Effects of Supplemental Instruction on Student Performance in a College-Level Mathematics Course." Paper presented at the American Educational Research Association Conference, San Francisco, Mar. 1989.

Kenney, P. A. "Effects of Supplemental Instruction on Student Performance in a College-Level Mathematics Course: A Report of Additional Results." Paper presented at the American Educational Research Association Conference, Boston, Apr. 1990.

Lundeberg, M. A. "Supplemental Instruction in Chemistry." *Journal of Research in Science Teaching,* 1990, *27* (2), 145–55.

Martin, D. C. "Learning Centers in Professional Schools." In K. V. Lauridsen, (ed.), *Examining the Scope of Learning Centers.* New Directions for College Learning Assistance, no. 1. San Francisco: Jossey-Bass, 1980.

Martin, D. C., Lorton, M., Blanc, R. A., and Evans, C. "The Learning Center: A Comprehensive Model for Colleges and Universities." Grand Rapids, Mich.: Aquinas College, 1977.

Martin, D. C., and Blanc, R. "The Learning Center's Role in Retention: Integrating Student Support Services with Department Instruction." *Journal of Developmental and Remedial Education,* 1980, *4* (2), 21–23.

Martin, D. C., and Arendale, D. R. (eds.). *Supplemental Instruction: Improving First-Year Student Success in High-Risk Courses.* Columbia, S.C.: National Resource Center for the Freshman Year Experience, University of South Carolina, 1992.

Martin, D. C., Blanc, R., and DeBuhr, L. "Supplemental Instruction: A Model for Student Academic Support." Kansas City, Mo.: University of Missouri, 1983.

National Council of Teachers of Mathematics. *Curriculum and Evaluation Standards for School Mathematics.* Reston, Va.: National Council of Teachers of Mathematics, 1989.

National Research Council. *Moving Beyond Myths: Revitalizing Undergraduate Mathematics.* Washington, D.C.: National Academy Press, 1991.

Pryor, S. A. "The Relationship of Supplemental Instruction and Final Grades of Students Enrolled in High-Risk Courses." Unpublished doctoral dissertation, Department of Education, Western Michigan University, 1989.

Skemp, R. R. *Intelligence, Learning, and Action: A Foundation for Theory and Practice in Education.* Chichester, UK: Wiley, 1980.

Wolfe, R. F. "The Supplemental Instruction Program: Developing Thinking and Learning Skills." *Journal of Reading,* 1987, *31* (3), 228–232.

PATRICIA ANN KENNEY is research associate at the University of Pittsburgh's Learning Research and Development Center.

JAMES M. KALLISON, JR., is director of Mathematics and Science Programs including Supplemental Instruction training at the Learning Skills Center, University of Texas at Austin.

A video-based delivery system using Supplemental Instruction offers a viable alternative to remedial course work, allowing underprepared students to excel in historically difficult courses as they develop needed basic skills.

VSI: A Pathway to Mastery and Persistence

Deanna C. Martin, Robert A. Blanc

In Chapter One of this volume, Gary Widmar describes the prevailing campus ethos at the University of Missouri–Kansas City (UMKC) at the time when the staff of the Center for Academic Development originated Supplemental Instruction (SI). Implicit in the faculty expectation (and explicit in the directions from administration) was the paradoxical dictum that the staff retain students without engaging in remedial activities. Supplemental Instruction satisfied the campus's immediate need by supporting high-risk courses rather than high-risk students.

Need for More Than Traditional Supplemental Instruction

Later, when UMKC joined Division I NCAA athletics, a group of students entered the university who were new to the campus: top flight and highly visible athletes. Although all met NCAA standards for admission, some demonstrated academic weakness; furthermore, they had to meet an extensive travel schedule that removed them from the campus at key points in the academic term.

Again, instructions from the administration (and the NCAA) seemed paradoxical. Although these students clearly faced problems that were unique on

The authors wish to acknowledge their debt to Clark Chipman, regional representative for Higher Education Grant Programs, Region V, for his support of SI and for the ideas he contributed to the creation of VSI, and to James S. Falls, associate professor of history, whose course at UMKC became the subject of the VSI experiment.

the campus, the academic support provided for them could not be categorically different from that available to others. It soon became evident to the center staff that SI, even with the addition of tutors at study tables (the standard regimen among Division I schools), was not sufficient to assure success for some athletes. Accordingly, staff undertook a reassessment of SI.

Limitations of Supplemental Instruction

What the staff realized as they reconsidered SI for seriously marginalized students was that the conventional model relied on students being able, with a modicum of proficiency, to perform four tasks:

1. Hear and understand the professor's language, and therefore the lecture
2. Read and understand the textbook and ancillary readings
3. Sit through a lecture and take some relevant notes
4. Write well enough to express ideas in an essay examination.

With the new population, it appeared that not all of the assumptions were valid. Nor were they valid for the other academically compromised students toward whom the university regularly made symbolic gestures: college-bound, central-city youth.

Staff resolved to develop a new, alternative course delivery system called VSI. This permutation of SI was based not on the professor's lecture, but rather on a videotape of the professor's lecture. The videotape mode provided many instructional advantages including student control over the rate of the flow of information, opportunity to monitor the quality of student comprehension as it occurred, direct integration of study skills and content, and the extended time needed to identify and correct both content and skill deficits.

If the new program worked, it could be used to address the needs of student athletes as well as the various populations of marginally prepared students. The staff had successfully used pieces of the proposed VSI model previously, and as they considered their experience as well as the research of others, they had reason to be hopeful.

Theories, Research, and Practices Behind VSI

Perhaps the single most basic bit of advice any academic lecturer receives is this: "First you tell them what you are going to tell them. Then you tell them. Then you tell them what you told them."

That bit of homely wisdom underlies several rather important approaches to student comprehension. For instance, both the Directed Reading Activity (Betts, 1946) and the Directed Reading-Thinking Activity (Stauffer, 1969) recognize that preparing students for learning is perhaps the most fundamental act in the teaching process. Robinson's (1961) SQ3R process formed the basis of college skill instruction for generations of students. This five-step process prefaces the reading experience with the *Survey* step and with the development of *Questions* that will guide the student's comprehension of the reading assignments to come. The student then *Read*(s) the material, followed by the *Recite* and *Review* steps. Thus another variant of the homely wisdom of the trade.

Variations on the same pedagogical theme were heard from teachers who recognized that five students working together can accomplish more than five students working independently of one another. The first on record with this view was Socrates. More recently, Whimbey and Sadler (1985) recommended "paired problem solving." Chemistry professor Carmichael (Whimbey and others, 1980) implemented a similar instructional style with students in the SOAR (Stress on Academic Reasoning) curriculum at Xavier University. Other science educators advocated like approaches: Karplus developed the Science Curriculum Improvement Study at Berkeley's Lawrence Hall of Science in the 1970s; Fuller (1980) followed a similar path in the ADAPT curriculum at the University of Nebraska. Lochhead and Clement (1979) developed the concept of *cognitive process instruction*. Austin (1961) found that increasing the frequency and quality of interaction between mathematics students and their teachers—and among students—produced gains in learning. Whimbey and Sadler (1985) encourage students to "think out loud." Empirical research verified intuition, and support grew for the idea of increasing opportunities for student interaction through collaborative learning techniques.

Prior Experience

In the early 1980s, the staff of the center, relying upon the materials and people cited above, developed applications of SI designed to answer the specific problem of medical students who failed the comprehensive examination in the basic sciences, which comes at the end of their second year. Later in the decade, when the number of students from all parts of the United States seeking admission to the UMKC Board Review program outstripped the available resources, the staff made a video-based program, *FIRSTprep*, available for adoption in medical schools outside Kansas City (Blanc, 1989). Although the video program was multifaceted, the central instructional procedure was relatively straightforward. The implementation steps that proved effective in *FIRSTprep* comprised the central core of VSI:

1. *Preview* both the vocabulary that will be used in the lecture and, in rather cursory fashion, the main topics to be covered in the lecture. ("Tell them what you are going to tell them.")

2. *Process* the videotaped lecture. In doing so, stop when necessary to permit students to clarify something the professor has said or simply to assure that the students are tracking the progress of the presentation. (This technique is derived from that used by John Madden, commentator on football for CBS network television, who likes to present plays in slow motion for the edification of his audience.) This is the "Tell them" phase of the lesson.

3. *Review* the videotaped lecture, using any of a variety of well-known techniques. ("Tell them what you told them.")

The difference between this approach and those traditionally used in post-secondary education lies in the centrality of students to the process as opposed to the centrality of the material to be learned:

• Students conduct the preview
• Students determine the pace of the lecture
• Students assure their own mastery as the lecture progresses
• Students select the key points for immediate review
• Students identify misconceptions and modify and adapt their conceptions to achieve, eventually, more complete understanding.

In essence, students take responsibility for their own learning. The role of the facilitator is to drag his or her feet, assuring that students understand the material while firmly resisting the pressure from students to give them answers, thus hurrying the process. In the final analysis, facilitators become experts in finessing answers from their groups.

The result of using videotaped lectures in this way was quite remarkable. In four years, the VSI method has been used with salutary effect by two dozen different medical schools and health care institutions, preparing people to perform well on medical boards. The combination of the three-stage presentation punctuated by student discussion has proved to be an extremely powerful learning mode.

Advice the Staff Rejected

A good deal of conventional wisdom operates among college reading and study skills programs. If students cannot read and understand a text, conventional wisdom tells us, first you must teach them to comprehend at least at the tenth-grade reading level. Then, they may be ready to enroll in a university course. Meanwhile, in order to help them develop the necessary basic skills, start them at the level where they are and move them at their own speed through the fundamentals of the elementary school, the middle school, and the high school.

What results come from educational programs designed to provide adults with basic skills? The answer proves somewhat disappointing. Those who go into developmental studies rarely matriculate in a university. The staff consulted one data base after another seeking evidence that adults who entered a developmental curriculum with skills at or below the middle school level had gone on to university level course work. They found only case studies which extolled the virtues of one or another student or of one or another teacher, or suggested methods that lacked rigorous evaluative data to support claims of effectiveness. Even today, research shows that only ten percent of African American students who participated in developmental programs at community colleges had either graduated or were still in school after a period of 3.5 years (Boylan, Bliss, and Bonham, 1993). Another recent study cites a 12 percent rate of persistence leading to enrollment in a senior institution if a student engaged in remedial course work. The latter figure is irrespective of ethnicity. Furthermore, editorials in abundance complain that students who enter programs of remedial course work lack the stamina to complete the course of study.

In discussion, staff came back again and again to an alternative view, arguing that lack of basic skills need not preclude a student's comprehension of an academic discipline. The example of Socrates was offered, and it proved persuasive. Staff were particularly responsive to Socrates' dialog with Meno in which, with Socrates' tutelage, an uneducated slave boy derives the Pythagorean Theorem. What was unusual about Socrates' students? By today's standards, they were surely underprepared. Yet with Socrates' guiding questions and his patient insistence that his students knew or could generate wise answers, they were able to invent the concepts of truth and justice that have survived intact to the present day. The next step was to create a fully integrated instructional system, which inextricably merged the learning process and the cognitive content of the discipline.

Original Instruction

Departing only slightly from *FIRSTprep*, staff devised VSI according to the following plan:

1. Get the most respected undergraduate professor who
2. Teaches one of the historically difficult courses.
3. Invite the professor into the video studio to deliver an entire course for the video camera.
4. Tidy the lectures with a modicum of editing.
5. Assign six hours of credit to the VSI block: three hours of regular history course credit and three hours of study skills credit.
6. Enroll at-risk students in a special section of the historically difficult course.
7. Give the students a videocassette recorder, a monitor, a blackboard, and a facilitator.
8. Arrange the schedules of the students to accommodate extended class periods.
9. Ask the professor to administer exams to the regular course and the video-based course on the same schedule and to apply the same grading standards to both sections of the course.
10. Present the video-based course with rigor equal to the regular course.
11. Having done all the foregoing, find a facilitator who has some familiarity with the material and train that person in techniques of collaborative learning.

In practice, VSI worked out exactly as planned. The professor had won the campus outstanding teacher award twice. His course in Western Civilization was definitely high risk with 20–30 percent of the students typically ending the semester with D or F grades or withdrawing prior to the end of the term. The professor would videotape the lectures and would cooperate in every way that had been outlined. In addition, he would meet periodically with the video-based class for one-half hour to answer questions.

VSI and Comparison Group

Lacking randomization and other key controls, this study can not claim to meet experimental criteria. The project, however, has been replicated with multiple groups over a period of five semesters on the UMKC campus, and lately on other campuses. The following set of data drawn from the Fall 1992 program is representative of the pilot studies conducted at UMKC. A comprehensive VSI study is in progress.

In the Fall of 1992, a total of 18 students enrolled in a special VSI section and 157 in the regular section of Western Civilization. Of the 157 students in the comparison group, 18 enrolled as "pass/no pass"; these were necessarily excluded from all comparisons regarding final course grades.

Regarding differences and similarities between the groups, campus experience has shown that professional school students are the most likely to persist; students who have not declared majors are least likely. The data revealed that the VSI group included one professional school student (5.6 percent) and 61 percent undeclared majors. The comparison group included 20 percent professional school students and only 39 percent undeclared majors. These differences were found to be statistically significant.

Varsity athletes, although not at risk for attrition, typically do not achieve grades as high as the average of students on campus. The VSI group enrolled 39 percent athletes; the comparison group, 4 percent. Minority ethnicity appears to be a risk factor on campus, and the VSI group enrolled 50 percent students of minority ethnicity compared with 25 percent in the comparison population. Only with respect to gender distribution and age were the two groups approximately the same.

None of the students in the VSI group had been on the dean's list for academic distinction; 13 percent of the other group had been so honored. Looking at probationary status, the reverse ratio appeared with 28 percent of the VSI group on academic probation and 12 percent of the comparison population showing this evidence of previous academic difficulty.

Early academic history revealed similar data: the VSI group entered the university with a mean ACT score of 16 and had graduated in the middle of their high school classes (52nd percentile). The comparison group earned mean scores of 25 on the ACT and graduated from their high schools in the 78th percentile.

Simply stated, those in the regular section of the Western Civilization course presented profiles that parallel those of academically successful students. The profiles of those in the VSI group would identify them as at-risk or underprepared according to multiple, accepted criteria.

Results

Results were examined with respect to several variables. Course grades are necessary but not sufficient measures of success. Whether the student persists in the university is as good or better a measure of success. Each of these was accepted as a dependent variable in assessing the effectiveness of the VSI project. Both measures indicated that the VSI group performed at as high a level or higher than the students in the regular lecture course.

Ninety-five percent of the VSI group earned A or B grades and none received D grades or failed. Fifty-three percent of students in the regular course received A or B grades, and 24 percent either received a D grade or failed. Final course grade average favored the VSI group with a mean of 3.6 (on a 4-point scale) compared with 2.3 for the comparison group.

With respect to reenrollment, all but one of the students in the VSI group and all of those on probation reenrolled for the following semester. Of those in the regular section, only 45 percent of the probationers and 85 percent overall returned to the university during the succeeding term.

In summary, by every available criterion, although the VSI group appeared to be at greater risk, their performance equaled or exceeded that of the regular lecture group.

The study skills pre- and post-test differences for the VSI group are still being analyzed. Students did show statistically significant gains in abstract reasoning, as measured by the Differential Aptitude Tests (Level 2, Form C) and by essay writing, as assessed by the course professor. Self-report data as shown on the FIRO-B, Learning and Study Strategies Inventory (LASSI), and the ACT ASSET revealed statistically significant gains in fifteen categories. Students demonstrated their ability to comprehend difficult material as they passed examinations dealing with their supplemental reading, which included Aristophanes' *Lysistrata*, Bolt's *A Man for All Seasons*, and Machiavelli's *The Prince*, all read in their entirety, along with essays by Cicero and others.

Discussion and Conclusion

The single most encouraging trend that emerges from the implementation of VSI as an alternative rather than a supplement to instruction is evidence that underprepared, at-risk students can master difficult and rigorous content and develop requisite skills at the same time. The corollaries of that statement are the following:

1. Students who cannot effectively read and understand the textbook or listen to and understand a professor's lecture or listen to a lecture and prepare a set of class notes can, nonetheless, learn history, and while doing so, can acquire or strengthen the skills necessary for academic success.
2. Students who cannot write an effective essay answer to an academic question can learn to do so within the context of an academic course of study.

These corollaries lead to the conclusion that students who are underprepared for postsecondary education can simultaneously engage in university study and develop the requisite skills.

Of equal importance perhaps is the obvious fact that the facilitator manages students' study time. VSI staff conclude that managed study is an essential component of the program, as students who are at-risk need direct support, at least until they are sufficiently practiced in the techniques of study to manage on their own.

Yet another implication of the VSI model relates to the centrality of the lecture in the educational process. In other, perhaps more literate times, the text was central to the learning experience, and the professor emphasized the elements of the text that were essential and linked those elements in insightful ways. Now, in response to a less literate generation, the lecture acquires the central instructional role with the text serving as reference material. It must be noted, however, that this reversal is only viewed by the VSI practitioner as temporary, that VSI holds promise as a means by which to move one to a higher level of literacy.

The magical ingredient in the process appears to be the technology, which manifests in the form of the videocassette and the remote control device. This technology enables the student to alternate between the professor's lecture and the silence in which to consider the meaning. The moments of silence are precious. Silence offers the student a rare commodity in the context of a classroom: time to think. And the reflective time allows the student to form questions, observations, and opinions. Those, then, are shared with fellow students. Confusion is resolved; conflicting views are weighed; differences are explored. Students leave the session with clearly defined questions and a sense of what to do next.

In the *Apology,* Plato quoted Socrates' statement: "The life which is unexamined is not worth living." The educational equivalent might be, "The lecture that is unexamined is not worth hearing." Adult students today, under the press of heavy commitments, rarely take time to actually examine and reflect upon what they are learning. Most feel fortunate if they can crowd in enough hours to meet the most immediate deadlines. In VSI, students have both the time and the guidance to examine not only the material of the discipline, but the ways in which they, as students, think and learn and interact with one another. Time and guidance may not be the characteristics of quick solutions, but they are more likely to be the characteristics of meaningful change.

References

Austin, M. "Improving Comprehension of Mathematics." In M. J. Weiss (ed.), *Reading in the Secondary Schools.* New York: Odyssey Press, 1961.

Betts, E. *Foundations of Reading Instruction.* New York: American Book, 1946.

Blanc, R. *FIRSTprep.* Institute for Professional Preparation, University of Missouri–Kansas City, 1989.

Boylan, H., Bliss, L., Bonham, B. "The Performance of Minority Students in Developmental Education." *Research in Developmental Education*, 1993, *10* (2), Appalachian State University, Boone, N.C.

Fuller, R. G. (ed.). *Piagetian Programs in Higher Education*. Lincoln, Neb.: ADAPT, 1980.

Karplus, R. *The Science Curriculum Improvement Study*. Berkeley: University of California Press, 1974.

Lochhead, J., and Clement, J. (eds.). *Cognitive Process Instruction*. Philadelphia: Franklin Institute Press, 1979.

Robinson, F. *Effective Study*. New York: HarperCollins, 1946.

Stauffer, R. *Directing Reading Maturity as a Cognitive Process*. New York: HarperCollins, 1969.

Whimbey, A., Carmichael, J. W., Jr., Jones, L. W., Hunter, J. T., and Vincent, H. A. "Teaching Critical Reading and Analytical Reasoning in Project SOAR." *Journal of Reading*, 1980, *24*, 5–10.

Whimbey, A., and Sadler, W. "A Holistic Approach to Improving Thinking Skills." *Phi Delta Kappan*, Nov. 1985, 199–203.

DEANNA C. MARTIN *is associate professor of education and director of the Center for Academic Development at the University of Missouri–Kansas City.*

ROBERT A. BLANC *is associate professor in the School of Medicine and director of the Institute for Professional Preparation at the University of Missouri–Kansas City.*

Index

ORDERING INFORMATION

NEW DIRECTIONS FOR TEACHING AND LEARNING is a series of paperback books that presents ideas and techniques for improving college teaching, based both on the practical expertise of seasoned instructors and on the latest research findings of educational and psychological researchers. Books in the series are published quarterly in spring, summer, fall, and winter and are available for purchase by subscription as well as by single copy.

SUBSCRIPTIONS for 1994 cost $47.00 for individuals (a savings of 25 percent over single-copy prices) and $62.00 for institutions, agencies, and libraries. Please do not send institutional checks for personal subscriptions. Standing orders are accepted.

SINGLE COPIES cost $15.95 when payment accompanies order. (California, New Jersey, New York, and Washington, D.C., residents please include appropriate sales tax.) Billed orders will be charged postage and handling.

DISCOUNTS FOR QUANTITY ORDERS are available. Please write to the address below for information.

ALL ORDERS must include either the name of an individual or an official purchase order number. Please submit your order as follows:
    Subscriptions: specify series and year subscription is to begin
    Single copies: include individual title code (such as TL54)

MAIL ALL ORDERS TO:
    Jossey-Bass Publishers
    350 Sansome Street
    San Francisco, CA 94104-1342

FOR SUBSCRIPTION SALES OUTSIDE OF THE UNITED STATES, CONTACT:
    any international subscription agency or Jossey-Bass directly.

Statement of Ownership, Management and Circulation
(Required by 39 U.S.C. 3685)

1A. Title of Publication	1B. PUBLICATION NO.	2. Date of Filing
NEW DIRECTIONS FOR TEACHING AND LEARNING	0 2 7 1 0 6 3 3	9/26/94

3. Frequency of Issue	3A. No. of Issues Published Annually	3B. Annual Subscription Price
Quarterly	Four (4)	$47.00 (personal) $62.00 (institutional)

4. Complete Mailing Address of Known Office of Publication *(Street, City, County, State and ZIP+4 Code) (Not printers)*

350 Sansome Street, 5th Flr, San Francisco, CA 94104-1342 (San Francisco Cnty)

5. Complete Mailing Address of the Headquarters of General Business Offices of the Publisher *(Not printer)*

(above address)

6. Full Names and Complete Mailing Address of Publisher, Editor, and Managing Editor *(This item MUST NOT be blank)*

Publisher *(Name and Complete Mailing Address)*

Jossey-Bass Inc., Publishers (above address)

Editor *(Name and Complete Mailing Address)*

Robert J. Menges, Northwestern Univ, 2115 N. Campus Dr, Evanston, IL 60208-2610

Managing Editor *(Name and Complete Mailing Address)*

Lynn D. Luckow, President, Jossey-Bass Inc., Publishers (address above)

7. Owner *(If owned by a corporation, its name and address must be stated and also immediately thereunder the names and addresses of stockholders owning or holding 1 percent or more of total amount of stock. If not owned by a corporation, the names and addresses of the individual owners must be given. If owned by a partnership or other unincorporated firm, its name and address, as well as that of each individual must be given. If the publication is published by a nonprofit organization, its name and address must be stated.) (Item must be completed.)*

Full Name	Complete Mailing Address
Simon & Schuster	PO Box 1172 Englewood Cliffs, NJ 07632-1172

8. Known Bondholders, Mortgagees, and Other Security Holders Owning or Holding 1 Percent or More of Total Amount of Bonds, Mortgages or Other Securities *(If there are none, so state)*

Full Name	Complete Mailing Address
same as above	same as above

9. For Completion by Nonprofit Organizations Authorized To Mail at Special Rates *(DMM Section 424.12 only)*
The purpose, function, and nonprofit status of this organization and the exempt status for Federal income tax purposes *(Check one)*

(1) Has Not Changed During Preceding 12 Months	(2) Has Changed During Preceding 12 Months	*If changed, publisher must submit explanation of change with this statement.*

10. Extent and Nature of Circulation *(See instructions on reverse side)*	Average No. Copies Each Issue During Preceding 12 Months	Actual No. Copies of Single Issue Published Nearest to Filing Date
A. Total No. Copies *(Net Press Run)*	1,819	1,765
B. Paid and/or Requested Circulation 1. Sales through dealers and carriers, street vendors and counter sales	520	303
2. Mail Subscription *(Paid and/or requested)*	770	890
C. Total Paid and/or Requested Circulation *(Sum of 10B1 and 10B2)*	1,290	1,193
D. Free Distribution by Mail, Carrier or Other Means Samples, Complimentary, and Other Free Copies	66	66
E. Total Distribution *(Sum of C and D)*	1,356	1,259
F. Copies Not Distributed 1. Office use, left over, unaccounted, spoiled after printing	463	506
2. Return from News Agents	0	0
G. TOTAL *(Sum of E, F1 and 2—should equal net press run shown in A)*	1,819	1,765

11. I certify that the statements made by me above are correct and complete	Signature and Title of Editor, Publisher, Business Manager, or Owner
	(signature) Larry Ishii Vice President

PS Form **3526,** January 1991   *(See instructions on reverse)*